Conway Urban Watershed Framework Plan

A Reconciliation Landscape for Little Creek-Palarm Creek Sub-watershed

University of Arkansas Community Design Center

ORO
EDITIONS

Preface

More than half of America's waterbodies are unsafe for swimming, fishing, and as sources of drinking water due to anthropogenic activity, mostly from city building and farming. Beyond water quality problems, dysfunctional streams cause flooding and erosion of property leading to neighborhood blight. Not only can this be reversed, but repair of degraded urban streams can be a powerful agent for reinventing the physical environments of post-industrial cities. This requires transdisciplinary collaboration between the fields of ecological engineering and urban design. Improved riparian (stream) corridors can provide premium urban land use frontage and greenways as linear parks—an entirely new category of urban space. The American city was uniquely premised on such fusions of landscape and urbanism—a tradition still with plenty of room for innovation given recent advancements in the ecological sciences.

Traditionally watershed plans have been an environmental engineering tool to guide improvements of hydrological functioning in watersheds through inventory, assessment, and correction. While such plans restore ecological services through sophisticated ecological engineering technologies, they have little to say about the city and urban design. Watershed plans, particularly USEPA Nine Element Plans, remain primarily data and policy-driven documents prepared by a professional subset with an important but singular interest in repairing waterbodies.

Conversely, urban planning has not codified the value of healthy ecosystems within which cities are built. In this age of the Anthropocene, when ecosystems are now human-dominated, resilient urban design must account for biological processes in constructing human habitat. Thus, the Conway Urban Watershed Framework Plan is a collaboration between ecological engineers and urban designers. The two project principals provide introductory essays framing their disciplines' roles in devising public interest design solutions. The Framework Plan introduces watershed management into urban design with one simple demand: that every new development investment contribute to watershed stewardship, where infrastructure and building deliver ecological services in addition to urban services. Otherwise, the costs of inaction will prove to be very high and unnecessary.

The Conway Urban Watershed Framework Plan formulates a planning vocabulary for use among professionals and decision makers to engage this new design market. Urban design recommendations are benchmarked to the 17 ecological services that all healthy ecosystems deliver. The stakes are high, as such recombinant design thinking will generate a truly pioneering, high-performing, and place-based public realm of great beauty.

Urban
Watershed
Planning
makes hard
engineering...

work more like soft engineering

offering the 17 ecosystem services

1. atmospheric regulation
2. climate regulation
3. disturbance regulation
4. water regulation
5. water supply
6. erosion control and sediment retention
7. soil formation
8. nutrient cycling
9. waste treatment
10. pollination
11. species control
12. refugia/habitat
13. food production
14. raw material production
15. genetic resources
16. recreation
17. cultural enrichment

Table of Contents

The Village at Hendrix, Conway

Introducing Watersheds, Cities, and Farms as Energy Systems

Stephen Luoni, Director
University of Arkansas Community Design Center

"….the principles of thermodynamics suggest that the most robust and resilient designs will not be based on the common notions of scarcity or conservation. Instead, the premise and goal of design should be exuberance, abundance, and excess, for the aim is the maximum of power and resilience of ecological and architectural formations through design."

Kiel Moe, ***Convergence: An Architectural Agenda for Energy***

As with many places experiencing growth, much unorganized energy flows through the City of Conway, causing a range of environmental dysfunctions. Streams flood, cities generate traffic congestion, industries pollute (often a toxic concentration of otherwise benign elements), and agriculture's organic wastes lead to algae blooms and the degradation of aquatic life downstream. Floods, congestion, pollution, and waste are unorganized energy concentrations. Such energy excesses signal both underperformance and potential in environmental systems. Rapid urbanization has overloaded Conway's urban streams with water volume, sediment, and nutrients exceeding the carrying capacities of its headwater streams to metabolize these inputs. Hardening of the watershed from impervious surfaces (streets, roofs, parking lots) accelerates drainage that floods, erodes property, scours streams, and multiplies dysfunctions collectively known as urban stream syndrome. The latter expresses degraded ecosystem structure with negligible ecological functioning. Meanwhile, downtown Conway's urban potential to provide viable neighborhoods and commerce are hindered by high water tables amplified by poor water management. Energy excesses, however, present design opportunities to improve performance among the three environmental systems: watersheds, cities, and farms. How then might urban design harness these energy excesses to create high quality places?

If energy, as architect Kiel Moe stipulates, "is the measure of a system's capacity to do work on its surrounding environment" (Moe: 21) then accordingly we would want to maximize useful work and ultimately maximize power, "the rate of flow of useful energy" (Odum: 32). Ideally, the work of energy in cities, watersheds, and farms leads to resilient functioning, maximizing system responsiveness to shifting growth and shrinkage scenarios. One measure of system productivity correlates to the level of services offered, or the maximum useful work. The role of design then is to enhance structure and performance among the three environmental systems in delivering sustained urban and ecological services. Ecological services involve higher order work related to soil structure and fertility, pollination, water quality and provisioning, genetic biodiversity, disturbance regulation, food provisioning, nutrient cycling, gas or atmospheric regulation, etc. (Costanza, et al: 253-260)—not traditionally the purview of urbanism. Despite that distressed ecosystems undermine economic and social performance in cities. Indeed, ecological problems are social problems. Such transformity—energy transferences from one environmental system to another to do higher quality work—will be explored later as a fundamental property of resilient communities.

The Conway Urban Watershed Framework Plan is premised on the transformation of energy excesses to enhance ecological and urban functioning. Funded by the USEPA, the immediate goal of the Framework Plan involves removal of the city's primary stream from Arkansas' Impaired Waterbodies List. Listed streams are too polluted or otherwise degraded to meet established water quality standards, due in Conway's case to ill-planned urbanization and organic waste discharges from urban agriculture. Planning recommendations are intended to prevent similar listing of the city's other four urban streams and Conway's premier lake, all on the cusp of an impairment designation. The Framework Plan mitigates further local watershed dysfunction through modulated planning initiatives to be undertaken by lay stakeholder groups and the city. Accordingly, we were not explicit about conceptual energy principles in framing recommended planning strategies illustrated in the book. Nevertheless, a summary introduction here of environmental energy principles as they relate to design offers design professionals a missing but necessary compass in urban design and planning. The Framework Plan was a collaboration between urban designers/architects and ecological engineers guided by the shared notion that watersheds, cities, and farms are energy systems governed by common principles of growth, maturation, and renewal. Such recombinant design thinking is essential since the greatest ongoing challenge in planning is design within, what are now, human-dominated ecosystems.

Energy should be a more explicit organizational precept in placemaking, beginning with the concept of succession. Succession is the process of system reset after a disruption. Resilient systems recover complex, redundant, feed-forward and feed-back dynamics after a system's upset (flood, fire, tornado, plowing, etc.). Studies in both urbanism and ecology teach us that systems transform their properties in their succession from pioneering (disrupted) to mature (stable) phases. Pioneering phases of developing systems are necessarily exploitative, energy excessive, unstructured, and low yield in their succession toward maturity. They do not yet have high connectivity, so exhibit unbalanced resource exploitation. Mature metropolises like New York and London were once collections of villages, while old growth forests began as low-diversity meadows. Their early expenditures of energy—whether for ecological, social, or economic work—were increasingly organized to produce higher orders of complexity. Complexity, or *climax* in systems thinking, is an energy state characterized by peak productivity despite lower levels of energy use, since systems always dissipate energy. While great cities and climax ecosystems like redwood forests individually exhibit complexity, the challenge remains how cities and ecosystems might achieve high-order functioning in the same space. This interdependence entails invention of planning interfaces to promote adaptive feedback between ecosystems and cities. Because city landscapes are always in some form of disruption, urban ecosystems must be explicitly designed to achieve complex resilience.

Understanding Resilience

Commonly held development paradigms like sustainability, regenerativity, complexity, and resiliency recast the discussion of environmental systems in terms of energy, though from divergent outlooks on self-design in ecosystems. Sustainability inclines toward austerity, steady-states, and sumptuary regulation in a permanent state of conservation. Conversely, resiliency and complexity acknowledge a non-linear horizon of transformations as energy pulses, organizes, and dissipates in its movement toward creating more durable structure. This particular outlook is key for understanding the implications of design intervention within different stages of a development (energy) hierarchy. Design can enhance structure and performance in environmental systems—watersheds, cities, and farms—as they evolve from favoring energy quantity to energy quality at the very moment energy is dissipating—the "maximum of power."

The maximum power principle anchors the systems-oriented thinking of ecologist Howard T. Odum, a pioneer in the fields of ecological engineering, environmental accounting, and energy systems language. Interestingly, Odum's work at the University of Florida from 1970 until his death in 2002 constituted a school of thought among a generation of architects, scientists, and ecological engineers who regularly collaborated in the 70s and 80s on city and ecosystem planning. Odum's final book, *Environment, Power, and Society for the Twenty-first Century: The Hierarchy of Energy*, synthesizes his development of energy systems concepts based on the integration of environment, thermodynamics, and economics. For our brief purposes then, three axioms surrounding Odum's notions on maximum power, energy hierarchy, and transformity inform our design and planning approach.

Maximum Power

"The maximum power principle explains why early succession minimizes diversity and later succession maximizes diversity. The first priority of a system is to maximize energy intake, to cover the area with energy receivers quickly, with units adapted for most rapid growth . . . The second priority is to maximize efficiency in its energy processing. When there are no excesses, unused resources to be found, a high diversity of cooperating units develops, with better efficiency and division of labor." (Odum: 56-57)

The Framework Plan highlights the role of ecological engineering to create the new urban pattern languages for maximum power. As our project colleague writes: "Ecological engineering is the process of designing systems that preserve, restore, and create ecosystem services. More succinctly, ecological engineers design ecosystem services, which are the goods and services humanity extracts from the ecosystem" (Matlock and Morgan: 1). Ecological engineering encodes the laws of nature into urbanization processes, advancing later-stage cooperation among systems of conservation (watersheds), development (cities), and cultivation (agriculture). Typical design projects undertaken by ecological engineers include design of wetland systems for water treatment and habitat, low impact development or ecologically-based stormwater management, riparian corridor improvements, urban ecosystems design and prototyping, and brownfield remediation. Each of these project types are incorporated into the Framework Plan's neighborhood planning, turning energy into social structure—an example of transformity discussed below.

Unfortunately, planning mindsets lack the energy perspectives necessary to address their communities' elevated metabolisms. Automobiles and hard-engineered urban stormwater drainage are Odum's "energy receivers" mentioned above, rapidly elevating metabolism in the early succession auto-dominant city and urbanized watershed. Conservation-minded remedies shunned the maximum power principle favoring instead anti-growth policies, sprawling low-density land use patterns, species-oriented preservation of negligible ecological yield, or export of energy imbalances (e.g., pollution, waste, traffic congestion) elsewhere. This burden-shift is characteristic of the modern conservation/preservation solution to complex challenges. For instance, hard-engineered stormwater systems composed of pond-and-pipe structures transport polluted water to another place without previous treatment, accelerating peak flow and flooding downstream neighbors. Conservation can unwittingly yield high-entropy systems that simply move problems around. Energy excesses were wasted information and design opportunities.

Energy Hierarchy
"Energy transformations form a series in which the output of one is the input to the next. Available energy decreases through each transformation, but the energy quality increases, with increased ability to reinforce energy interactions upscale and downscale . . . With increasing scale, storage increase, depreciation decreases, and pulses are stronger but less frequent." (Odum: 63)

If we consider Conway's sub-watershed areas to be low-diversity, high-energy systems marked by unruly flooding, erosive energy, and nutrient overloading, how might design transform watershed structure toward higher order functioning? The concentration of water and its inherent energy is an opportunity to structure a durable treatment and storage network around wetlands, floodplains, stream and lake reclamation sites, greenways, and green streets. These infrastructure components constitute Odum's "diversity of cooperating units" in a new division of labor toward a higher order. Likewise, roads, trails, and parking lots can be designed to deliver ecological services using treatment based streetscapes to metabolize pollutants in stormwater runoff, a higher order functioning possible only through green infrastructure.

Or, what if existing farms supported by industrial inputs from fertilizer, herbicides, and pesticides adopted permaculture growing principles that prevent nutrient overloading and sedimentation of bordering streams? "Eco-farming" rebuilds soil health employing plant companioning to maximize diversity and nutrient exchange, while facilitating integrated pest management to elevate self-organization and resilience.

Scientists argue that soil made from rich biotic communities can potentially reverse global warming due to soil's unrivalled capacity to sequester carbon (see Ohlson). Instead of using ten calories to produce one calorie of food as current industrial farming does, permaculture reverses energy inefficiencies wherein farming could once again use one calorie to produce ten calories of food. Eco-farming also advances stream health through creation of vegetated stream buffers and farm wetlands to grow food and store excess nutrients while improving water quality and aquatic biodiversity. Wetlands are important energy reservoirs and genetic banks that amass energy from pulsing flood cycles to regulate stream metabolism and watershed functioning. Categorically the second most productive landscapes on Earth behind rain forests in terms of biomass, efficient nutrient cycling, and energy flow (Campbell and Ogden: 47), wetlands also deliver additional cultural and recreational functions important to urban quality of life. Each farm becomes an ecosystem.

Akin to energy capture in wetlands, riparian corridors—and street right-of-ways for that matter—are reconceptualized as "rain terrains" rather than drainage systems for evacuating water. Hard engineering simplifies the line of the stream's drainage function subverting the intrinsic ecological services and disturbance regulation offered by streams, thus amplifying risks to Conway. In contrasting channeled rivers to their conception of the rain terrain as a working storehouse, architects Anuradha Mathur and Dilip da Cunha are implicitly projecting an energy hierarchy.

> "In a rain terrain, on the other hand, rain does not flow: it overflows after being held where it falls in interstices, pores, fields, depressions, terraces, wells, snow fields, and glaciers, until it exceeds the capacity of that particular holding. It is then held again in a more extended realm, and so on, moving in emergent and transfiguring, non-linear and field-like ways that cannot be confined within lines as flows can. This is particularly the case given that overflows move not just in complex ways across the earth; they also move in complex times." (Mathur and da Cunha: 9)

Through facultative geometry, flow, and concentrated material, forms of potential energy in water can be harvested to organize higher levels of urban work, providing the community with critical ecological services. Ecological or ecosystem services are life-affirming resources and processes supplied by healthy natural ecosystems and serve all living organisms. The 17 recognized ecosystem services are grouped into four categories of **Provisioning Services** related to food, fiber, and fuel, **Regulating Services** supportive of climate regulation, and soil and water protection, **Supporting Services** affect soil structure, water cycling, genetic stores, and **Cultural Services** (Matlock and Morgan: 264). Ecosystem services highlight the role of transformity in environmental energy systems—transference of benefits from one system to the next.

Transformity

"... large quantities of low-quality energy are the basis for but controlled by small quantities of high-quality energy... Transformity is defined as the calories of available energy of one form previously required directly and indirectly to generate one calorie of another form of energy." (Odum: 73)

The prospect that design can organize energy excesses in early stage succession to deliver higher order ecological and urban services later makes a strong case for the role of transformity in urban planning. If ecological problems are social problems, then ecological solutions can steer social and economic solutions indispensable to future placemaking. Urban ecosystems—a critical element in bioregions—will drive the next economy. As John Thackara writes in his *How to Thrive in the Next Economy,* "A bioregional approach reimagines the man-made world as being one element among a complex of interacting, codependent ecologies: energy, water, food, production, information. It attends to flows, biocorridors, and interactions. It thinks about metabolic cycles and the 'capillarity' of the metropolis wherein rivers and biocorridors are given pride of place." (29)

For example, a riparian corridor that routinely floods may be reconfigured as a rain terrain, changing destructive channel flows to laminar flows that in their eddies and meandering geometries seed new landscapes as productive energy sinks. These nutrient sinks soon develop microbial-rich hydric soils with biodiverse and floristic wetland plant communities housing robust wildlife habitat, all from cyclic but non-disruptive flooding. Nutrient sinks or wetlands might sponsor new pollinator parks, or flyways that attract birdwatching, or new fishing holes. Sinks could serve as nodes for new types of conservation-oriented neighborhoods connected by bicycle/ pedestrian trail systems and green streets, featuring connectivity to schools. Private yards could be xeriscapes (drought tolerant landscapes) that complement wetland plant communities to elevate the level of ecological service from the traditional turf lawn, including aesthetics (less expensive and less maintenance!). Neighborhood streets as rain terrains manage water ecologically, that in turn, calm traffic to reclaim a safe and social environment for gathering within the space of the street. Streets can once again be place-based stages for public life as they deliver non-traffic social services without sacrificing traffic flow. A viable alternative to motorized transportation, greenways organize flows in water, material, food, and transportation to form a resilient municipal open space system. Greenways everywhere are attracting their own mixed land use development for residents who want to front a non-motorized public right-of-way. Their edges are creating value akin to that of waterfronts. Hence, the natural capital in nutrient sinks enhances economic development opportunities. Ironically, this scenario describes highly desirable urban vacation spots and high-income neighborhoods. We seem to desire the vitality that comes from connectivity and expressions of wholeness when we vacation.

Our ecological engineering collaborators caution us that: "The impact of land use change on biodiversity will likely be larger than that of climate change" (Matlock and Morgan: 12). Indeed, greater understanding of the value in ecological services will likely translate into more clustered land uses with better energy accounting and new kinds of places that deliver ever greater levels of livability for lower costs. Like in late succession development, cooperation will underwrite new forms of ecological, economic, and social (including equitability) functioning if we are mindful enough to steward their transformations. Designing within the Anthropocene, the era of human-dominated ecosystems, requires that we develop the vocabularies and toolkits for reconciling urban ecosystems and the geological force that is mankind.

References

Campbell, Craig and Michael Ogden. *Constructed Wetlands in the Sustainable Landscape,* John Wiley & Sons, Inc., 1999.

Costanza, Robert, Ralph D'Arge, Rudolf De Groot, Stephen Farber, Monica Grasso, Bruce Hannon, Karin Limburg, Shahid Naeem, Robert O'Neill, Jose Paruelo, Robert Gaskin, Paul Sutton, and Marjan Van Den Belt. "The value of the world's ecosystem services and natural capital", *Nature,* 387 (May 15, 1997).

Mathur, Anuradha and Dilip da Cunha. *Design in the Terrain of Water,* Applied Research + Design Publishing with the University of Pennsylvania, School of Design, 2014.

Matlock, Marty and Robert Morgan. *Ecological Engineering Design: Restoring and Conserving Ecosystem Services,* John Wiley & Sons, Inc., 2011.

Moe, Kiel. *Convergence: An Architectural Agenda for Energy,* Routledge, 2013.

Odum, Howard T. *Environment, Power, and Society for the Twenty-First Century: The Hierarchy of Energy,* Columbia University Press, 2007.

Ohlson, Kristin. *The Soil Will Save Us: How Scientists, Farmers, and Foodies are Healing the Soil to Save the Planet,* Rodale Books, 2014.

Thackara, John. *How to Thrive in the Next Economy: Designing Tomorrow's World Today,* Thames & Hudson, 2015.

Urban Eco-Hydrology: Designing Resilience for Human Systems

Marty D. Matlock, Ph.D., Director
University of Arkansas Office for Sustainability

Humanity is a hydraulic species. We have settled on the banks of rivers and shores of lakes and oceans, where we have access to fresh water, for 10,000 years (Kottak: 11). Water is life – it is our first need as individuals and as civilizations. Our cities utilize water for fisheries, transportation, waste disposal, even burial of our dead (Wohl: 1). Our cities grew from the oxbows and banks of great rivers, and many smaller water bodies around the world. So it is with Conway, Arkansas. Perched above the Arkansas River, one of the Mississippi River's great tributaries, Conway is a model city for exploring resilience in urban hydrology.

Resiliency, a concept from systems ecology, is the ability of a system to recover its structure and functionality after disturbance. This is the fundamental characteristic of a sustainable system (Folke, et al: 2). Resilient systems have complex networks of interconnected and interacting elements. These elements create redundancy of function and structure, diversity within the pathways and mechanisms of critical functions, buffers to perturbation, and the ability to recover functionality after disturbance (Berkes and Turner: 479).

A city is a social-ecological system (SES) where people and ecosystem processes are interdependent. For cities, adaptability and transformability are prerequisites to resilience (Folke, et al: 5). Adaptability is the capacity of the human and ecological elements of the system to change based upon knowledge, experience, internal processes and external forces. Adaptability requires a capacity to understand change, integrate new models of decision-making, and alter internal processes to drive outcomes. Transformability is the capacity of the city to change the order of interactions to create a new organizational structure for decision-making. Transformability does not mean the entire social network has to be able to change; rather, changes in small systems can drive transformation of the overall system. Eco-hydrology design elements provide a new approach to managing hydrologic systems as interconnected elements rather than discrete phenomena, and create the language necessary for adapting decision processes. These relatively small changes in design strategies for urban hydrology have the potential to transform municipal decision processes across other areas of management.

Cities across the U.S. are struggling to manage changing land use impacts within their watersheds, changing hydrology from increased frequency and intensity of extreme events, and increased demands on water resources for industrial, municipal, and recreational uses. These challenges are compounded by residential demand for urban quality of life. The standard framework for water resource management in the U.S. is to regulate water based upon discrete uses or impacts. The Clean Water Act[1] (CWA) regulates discharges of pollutants into surface waters of the U.S.; these include point sources such as wastewater treatment plants and industries. However, nonpoint sources (rainfall runoff) regulations are limited to urban stormwater, and those are relatively weak in implementation. Water quality for human consumption is regulated under the Safe Drinking Water Act[2] (SDWA), which protects water

---

[1]   33 U.S.C. §1251 et seq. (1972)
[2]   42 U.S.C. §300f et seq. (1974)

quality for designated drinking water uses. These regulations are composed of a patchwork of permitting criteria that address discrete elements of water resource management; watershed-level resource management is rare in the United States. The USEPA recognizes the incongruences in national regulations, and has provided funding for development for watershed plans across the U.S. to reduce water resource conflict and improve water quality. The USEPA National Nonpoint Source Management Program (CWA subsection 319) provides over $160 million per year to states and tribes to develop watershed strategies for managing water quality at the watershed level. These funds are limited to support restoration rather than protection of water bodies; this is a major policy failure by USEPA. Cities must have resources and authority to protect un-degraded water bodies, rather than only restoring degraded systems. Protecting urban water resources means protecting the ecological integrity of the watershed from land use change. Lake Conway receives water from all five sub-watersheds within the City of Conway; all five systems must function effectively if water resources are to be protected and restored.

Eco-hydrologic approach considers the entire watershed as the driver for water quantity and quality at the watershed outlet (Zalewski: 825-834). This approach explicitly understands the interrelations between water flow, nutrient dynamics, habitat modification, biodiversity, and land use within the watershed. Eco-hydrology can create resilience in cities by reducing damages from extreme events while enhancing ecosystem services across the urban landscape (Matlock and Morgan: 68). The eco-hydrologic approach provides a more coherent way to understand and manage water resources in rapidly changing conditions. This approach incorporates the following three principles (Zalewski: 825-834):
1. Hydrologic principle: the hydrodynamics of a watershed as impacted by climate change will define the risks of disruption from extreme events and opportunities for restoration after extreme events.
2. Ecological principle: hydrologic ecosystem resilience can be understood through the land use history and geography of the ecosystem.
3. Ecological engineering principle: enhancement of ecosystem resistance/resilience can be designed using systems thinking integrated with stakeholder engagement.
The watershed is the most logical unit of management for water resources, yet municipal jurisdictions rarely align with watershed boundaries. The fundamental structure of the decision processes within urban authorities is divorced from hydrologic realities. Regional authorities, which in the U.S. are much weaker than municipal authorities, are similarly disconnected from watershed boundaries. Our impacts on watershed hydrology result from direct modifications to the stream and stream corridor and modifications of land use and land cover in the watershed, creating the suite of problemscapes faced by the City of Conway. These problemscapes can be categorized as hydrologic regime modification, habitat degradation, and water pollution.

When management begins at the watershed scale, water resource becomes the focal point and managers develop a more complete understanding of overall conditions in the area and the stressors affecting those conditions (EPA, 1996). Management from the watershed level allows the manager and ecological engineer to consider factors beyond chemical pollution in protecting water quality. These factors include habitat destruction, geomorphologic changes, and changes in land use. The purpose behind USEPA's nine element watershed planning program is to begin to create this systems-level approach. However, the fragmented nature of water resource regulations in the U.S. limits the effectiveness of this plan. Of the five sub-watersheds in Conway, only Stone Dam Creek is listed by USEPA as impaired, and thus eligible for funding for protection and remediation.

Creating resilient eco-hydrologic systems within cities requires stakeholder engagement since many of the activities and infrastructure elements must be constructed and managed on private lands. The USEPA envisions municipalities engaging stakeholders across the political spectrum to implement watershed management plans. This process reinforces social networks so that when disruptions to urban infrastructure occur, the critical services necessary to support human life and prosperity can be restored rapidly (Pataki, et al: 341-347). We applied the Collaborative Learning process of stakeholder engagement to develop the Conway watershed plan (Sabatier, et al: 6). Stakeholders were recruited to represent key organizations, including city management, industry, residential groups, conservation organizations, regional planning, state environmental agencies, and agricultural organizations. Stakeholder meetings were convened quarterly over a three-year period to create a common understanding of Conway's water issues across each stakeholder sector. Stakeholders worked through priority concerns such as urban flooding, bank erosion, sediment loading and water quality in Lake Conway, as well as other issues. These stakeholder deliberations drove the development of the Conway Urban Watershed Framework Plan, an eco-hydrologic approach to addressing these problems.

The primary issue with land use modification is that it changes the ecosystem, causing cascading effects downstream. In some areas, most of the native landscape matrix has been replaced by agriculture, leaving native vegetation only in patches. Tillage and soil compaction interfere with the soil's capacity to regulate the flow of water in the landscape. Surface runoff may increase, and the soil's water-holding capacity may be decreased. Increased erosion and sediment transport are common. Other aspects of agriculture such as irrigation and field drainage also alter the natural hydrology of the watershed. Finally, applied chemicals such as fertilizer, pesticides, and herbicides may leach into the groundwater or wash off in surface runoff. All of these activities drive water resource degradation, yet are managed incrementally if at all within typical urban systems. The primary axiom of systems ecology is everything is connected.

Assessing and improving the resilience of urban systems requires a common set of indicators. Cutter, et al., (5) proposed five categories of indicators for resilience for urban eco-hydrology: Social, Economic, Institutional, Infrastructure, and Community Capital. The problemscapes identified in the Conway Urban Watershed Framework Plan are appropriate metrics for an eco-hydrology indicator for resilience. Collectively, the resulting six indicators of urban resilience constitute a coherent body of information to support adaptability and transformability within urban systems (Table 1). Designing resilient urban ecoscapes is a significant challenge. Each eco-hydrology design element for adaptive infrastructure supports many of the indicators of resilience for urban systems. For example, the lake restoration element serves the economic indicator by supporting eco-tourism and enhancing property values. The Green Streets and Park and City Greenway serve the social indicator by increasing community connectivity. The urban eco-farm supports the social, economic, and community capital indicators by increasing property value through aesthetic planning, enriched community engagement by connecting public spaces, and improved quality of life. This integrated approach amplifies the value of each design element, transforming the way citizens understand their cities.

Designing cities that are resilient in the face of the rapid changes expected in the next 50 years is not easy. Catastrophic damages from extreme weather events are costing U.S. cities billions of dollars in property damages and disruption of commerce. Applying the principles of eco-hydrology illustrated in this watershed plan could reduce the impacts from flooding, improve water quality, and enhance the quality of life for residents. The elements of eco-hydrologic design support social, economic, and institutional infrastructure within communities, promoting adaptive and transformational urban institutions. Designing urban eco-hydrologic elements at the watershed scale will create more resilient, sustainable, and livable cities.

References

Berkes, F. and N.J. Turner. "Knowledge, learning and the evolution of conservation practice for social ecological system resilience", *Human Ecology*, 34(4), 2006.

Cutter, S.L., C.G. Burton, and C.T. Emrich, "Disaster resilience indicators for benchmarking baseline conditions", *Journal of Homeland Security and Emergency Management*, 7(1), 2010.

Dalziell, E.P. and S.T. McManus. "Resilience, vulnerability, and adaptive capacity: implications for system performance", 2004. Presented at the International Forum for Engineering Decision-Making (IFED), Soos, Switzerland, December 6-8, 2004. Available at: https://ir.canterbury.ac.nz/handle/10092/2809.

Folke, C., S.R. Carpenter, B. Walker, M. Scheffer, T. Chapin, and J. Rockstrom. "Resilience thinking: integrating resilience, adaptability and transformability". *Ecology and Society* 15(4): 20.3, 2010.

Kottak, C.P. "Window on humanity", *Urban Anthropology*, 11, 2004.

Matlock, Marty and Robert Morgan. *Ecological Engineering Design: Restoring and Conserving Ecosystem Services,* John Wiley & Sons, Inc., 2011.

Pataki, D.E., C.G. Boone, T.S. Hogue, G.D. Jenerette, J.P. McFadden, and S. Pincetl. "Socio-ecohydrology and the urban water challenge", *Ecohydrology*, 4(2), 2011.

Sabatier, P., W. Focht, M. Lubell, Z. Tracthenberg, A. Vedletz, and M. Matlock, Eds. *Swimming Upstream: Collaborative Approaches to Watershed Management*, The MIT Press, 2005.

Wohl, E. *A World of Rivers: Environmental Change on Ten of the World's Great Rivers*, University of Chicago Press, 2010.

Zalewski M. "Ecohydrology – the use of ecological and hydrological processes for sustainable management of water resources", *Hydrological Sciences Journal*, 47(5), 2002.

Table 1: Indicators of Resilience for Urban Systems (modified from Cutter et al., 2010).

Resilience Indicator	Metrics
1. Social	A. Educational Equity B. Age demographics C. Transportation D. Health Care E. Connections to community
2. Economic	A. Housing capital B. Employment C. Income and equality D. Employment Diversity E. Health Access
3. Institutional	A. Flood coverage B. Municipal services C. Political access D. Disaster History E. Social connectivity
4. Infrastructure	A. Housing types B. Housing age C. Shelter capacity: needs D. Evacuation potential E. Recovery infrastructure
5. Community Capital	A. Place attachment B. Political engagement C. Social capital: religion D. Social capital: advocacy E. Change Culture - Innovation history
6. Eco-Hydrology	A. Hydrologic modification B. Percent impervious C. Riparian corridor connectedness D. Habitat intactness E. Water quality

re-imagining Conway

From existing scrap yard on Markham Street

... to proposed Neigborhood Town Square on Markham Street

Executive Summary

" Where two distinct types of network meet, flow slows down to diffusion. This is where the network structure is most vulnerable—and interestingly where living processes occur. "

Michael Mehaffy and Nikos Salingaros
Design for a Living Planet: Settlement, Science, and the Human Future

The City and the Watershed: A Reconciliation Landscape

How can city form fix the watershed? The city and the watershed are distinct systems of flow that generate shape and structure across the landscape to maximize their intrinsic objectives. The city, consisting of a place's street fabric, neighborhoods, and buildings, is a flow network designed to facilitate human social and economic exchange. Despite a bewildering variation in form, livable cities deliver *urban services* related to housing, mobility, and commerce usually at densities that minimize nature's presence and the underlying benefits from its biological processes. Cities, like all flow systems, tend to evolve into ever more efficient configurations inclined to privilege the specialized currents that pass through them—in this case, cars, people, and goods.

Likewise, the watershed's flow system, consisting of a catchment area's streams and lakes, is a flow network modeled by hydrological and biological processes. Akin to all healthy ecosystems, watersheds deliver the 17 life-affirming *ecosystem services* that underpin our collective economic and individual well-being, including pollination, atmospheric regulation, food production, nutrient cycling, maintenance of a genetic pool, disturbance regulation, water quality, flood and erosion control, soil health, etc. As streams, or *riparian corridors*, feed larger streams their channels and floodplains require more undisturbed land area with complex biotic communities of healthy soil structure, plant guilds, and wildlife chains to support ecological functioning. The ecosystem services framework is a fundamental benchmark for reconnecting streams' normative sediment and water flows to Lake Conway, while assessing the overall quality of interactions among natural and social infrastructure. How might city form play a role in restoring lost ecological services?

Streams, like streets, buildings, or any complex system for that matter, possess their own architecture comprised of components with specialized purposes toward a functioning whole (see Typical Riparian Corridor Cross-Section). All natural streams, from the first order stream like the ones in this sub-watershed to a 10th order stream like the Mississippi River, have a *bankfull* (stream proper), a sinuous path with alternating erosional and depositional zones, and

*terms in italics are included in glossary at end of the report

a floodplain 10-30 times the width of the bankfull (at its widest point the Mississippi River floodplain would be 10-30 miles wide). Before improved environmental regulations in the 1970s, floodplains were typically the first stream organs eliminated in urbanization. Watersheds, like cities then, thrive by way of their own specialized throughputs. *Hence, watersheds in urban areas are in direct competition with cities over the very ways in which the surface area should be shaped.*

Where the flow systems of the city and the watershed meet—their *ecotone*—arise the greatest dysfunctions. Peak stormwater flows into streams after rainfalls compound downstream flooding and erosion, leading to recurrent property damage and permanent decline in value. Riparian corridors in cities often exhibit what ecologists call *urban stream syndrome.* Here, stream metabolism as measured by flow energy and sediment transport is so elevated beyond its norm that streams lose their capacity to function as ecological systems, simply becoming destructive conduits for moving the city's pollution

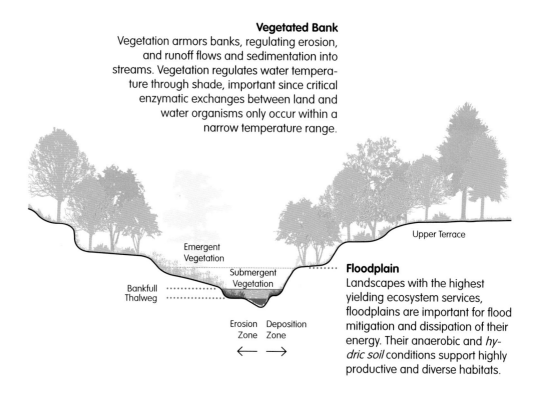

Vegetated Bank
Vegetation armors banks, regulating erosion, and runoff flows and sedimentation into streams. Vegetation regulates water temperature through shade, important since critical enzymatic exchanges between land and water organisms only occur within a narrow temperature range.

Upper Terrace

Emergent Vegetation

Submergent Vegetation

Bankfull
Thalweg

Erosion   Deposition
Zone   Zone

← →

Floodplain
Landscapes with the highest yielding ecosystem services, floodplains are important for flood mitigation and dissipation of their energy. Their anaerobic and *hydric soil* conditions support highly productive and diverse habitats.

Typical Riparian Corridor Cross-Section

around. ***Keep in mind that the first hour of urban stormwater runoff can have a pollution index far higher than that of raw sewage.*** Much of this is due to urban runoff's concentrations of *hydrocarbons* and metals, residues of the automobile and fertilizer industries captured during the *first flush*. Additionally, research shows that more than 10 percent coverage of surface area with hard—*impervious*—surfaces from roofs, parking lots, and roads can lead to regional watershed damage, while more than 30 percent coverage can lead to irreversible watershed destruction. The resulting 'flashy' hydrologic cycles yield chronic and expensive environmental impairments difficult to correct.

Where the city and the watershed meet also presents the greatest opportunities for creative development solutions reconciling the demands of each. Thus, new development patterns should appear. The land-water interface is Earth's most productive ecotone with the greatest degree of nutrient exchange and novel life forms arising exclusively within the seam of these two media. Conventional civil engineering has never known how to embrace this seam between city and water, the *hard* and the *soft*, or the artificial and the ecological. Conventional hard-engineered drainage solutions are costly, and their sole function to evacuate polluted water imposes a low return on investment while compounding regional watershed dysfunction. ***Herein lies the planning challenge for cities in wet places: to develop an urban infrastructure that simultaneously solves for ecologically-based water management while facilitating the city's functioning and growth.*** Some cities, like Austin, have adopted a "non-degradation clause" into their water management plans, requiring that new development not affect water quality. This expanded definition of utility entails a hybrid hard/soft infrastructure incorporating principles of natural hydrology that delivers both ecological and urban services in one infrastructure. This expanded definition of utility also entails multiple returns on investment, the only fiscally responsible approach to ongoing infrastructure funding challenges. Infrastructure for the 21st century city will simply have to do more work.

The Framework Plan: Develop a Representative Cityscape for Conway

The City of Conway, the state's second fastest growing city in the nation's 75th fastest growing county (out of 3,143 counties and county-equivalents in the U.S.) resides in the eastern portion of the Lake Conway-Point Remove Watershed. Lake Conway-Point Remove Watershed was designated a 2011-2016 Priority Watershed by the Arkansas Natural Resources Commission. The Conway

Urban Watershed Framework Plan is part of a larger USEPA funded initiative to mitigate water quality problems in the Little Creek-Palarm Creek sub-watershed incorporating the urbanized area of Conway. The sub-watershed drains approximately 42 square miles and contains two major streams of concern, Stone Dam Creek and Little Creek, both exhibiting urban stream syndrome. The immediate goal is to enact steps leading to the removal of Stone Dam Creek from the Arkansas Department of Environmental Quality 2010 *303(d) list of impaired water bodies* due to ammonia and nitrate concentrations from a municipal source. Downstream sedimentation and nutrient loading are contributing to the continued decline of Lake Conway. A major natural and economic asset to the area, Lake Conway at 6,700 acres is the largest reservoir built by a game and fish commission in the United States. Conway's current urbanization patterns, mostly low-density, automobile-oriented development, are incompatible with the sustained hydrological functioning of Lake Conway.

The Conway Urban Watershed Framework Plan focuses on the seam between city and water to create a **reconciliation landscape**. Imagine a cityscape that cultivated an amenity-rich, highly livable green urban environment made through "low-tech/high concept" enhancements to ordinary infrastructure investments already scheduled to service the city's growth. **To that end, the Framework Plan proposes a portfolio of value-added infrastructural retrofits—green streets, water treatment art parks, urban eco-farms, conservation neighborhoods, parking gardens, riparian corridor improvements, lake aerators, vegetative harvesters and floating bio-mats, and a city greenway—complementing mainstream infrastructural investments** (see Adaptive Infrastructure). Each retrofit type—or adaptation—offers operational competencies in a planning framework responsive to the urban environment's complexities. While the immediate objective is to restore ecological functioning in impaired water bodies, eventually removing Stone Dam Creek from the impaired water bodies list, a legacy in building a high-quality, *resilient* green public realm is the greater long-term objective. Here, building a representative cityscape expressive of the city's rising growth and status through a highly-productive civic green utility is within easy grasp for Conway.

Sponge City Gradient: City and Watershed Interfaces
Cities are discrete, whereas nature is inherently continuous. Optimal ecosystem functioning entails **physical connectivity among landscapes**—the very quality urbanization tends to erase. In downtown Conway with impervious

Stream Channelization leads to high headwater velocity while eliminating stream components: thalweg, bankfull, and floodplain, which deliver ecological services.

Steep banks and concrete armoring accelerates urban runoff and sediment discharges; the riparian edge delivers no ecological services in this hard engineered flow segment.

Conventional Hard Engineering

Corridor exhibits healthy stream sinuosity known as *riffle-pool-glide*: an algorithm of alternating shallow and deep areas in the stream base flow (thalweg). Wiers and fish ladders are part of beneficial hard/soft hybrid engineering.

Hendrix Creek Preserve, Conway - Soft Engineering

surface averaging more than 50 percent coverage, opportunities for implementing ecologically-based infrastructure adaptations are highly localized and sporadically distributed. Alternatively, riparian corridors and land-rich suburban development readily accommodate large-scale retrofits characterized by high connectivity for optimal ecological functioning. Nonetheless, all sectors of the city, whether high density development or undeveloped sites, hold capacities for water management that contribute to healthy watershed functioning. Aligning such capacities is a matter of design. ***The city can be engineered to work like a sponge.***

The Sponge City Gradient (see diagram) illustrates the structural interfaces between land use characteristics (i.e., function, intensity, and surrounding development patterns) and natural hydrology in the city-nature continuum. Since land uses offer radically uneven opportunities for water management, ecological infrastructure is accordingly configured to network within prevailing development profiles shaping downtown, suburban, exurban, and rural territories. Four typological configurations recognize these cross-sectional differences. ***Pixelation*** works within fragmented and hardened downtown landscapes. ***Nesting*** engages the pulsed frequencies of activity in parking lots and other large commercial sites. ***Clustering*** is an ideal pattern language for land-rich development. ***Connection*** in rural areas and along riparian corridors continues the imperative that large-scale natural systems connect. The gradient's usefulness as a general planning tool is complemented by attention to specific ecological-based water treatment technologies incorporating both mechanical and biological techniques.

The Six Water Management and Treatment Technologies

The hydrological design objective is to ***slow, soak,*** and ***spread*** urban runoff through landscape systems, given their intrinsic capacity for biologic treatment and metabolization of contaminants. Whereas urban runoff management for most cities has entailed a hard-engineered drainage network designed primarily for flood protection and quick evacuation of water, soft engineering approaches using landscapes employ ***flow attenuation***, ***filtration***, ***infiltration***, ***detention***, ***retention***, and ***bioremediation*** with better management results while achieving collateral environmental benefits (see Water Treatment Technologies diagram). Both soft and hard engineering techniques can be assembled as customized landscapes employing a combination of Low Impact Development, riparian corridor improvements, and green urban infrastructure.

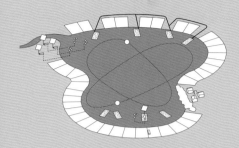

Lake Restoration

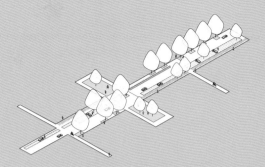

Green Streets and Parks

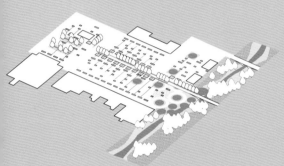

Parking Gardens

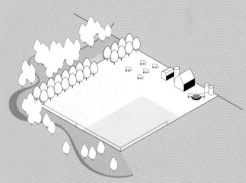

Urban Eco-Farm

Conservation Development

City Greenway

Adaptive Infrastructure

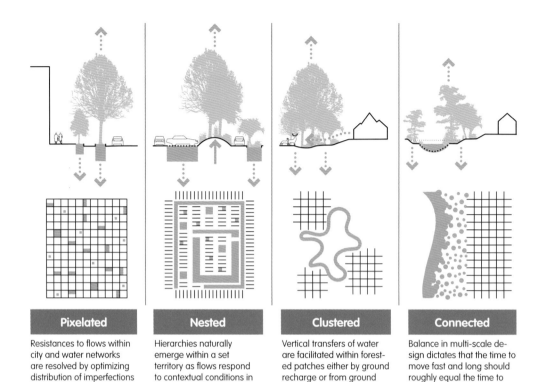

Pixelated	Nested	Clustered	Connected
Resistances to flows within city and water networks are resolved by optimizing distribution of imperfections throughout the system. Optimization is addressed through localized treatment facilities within dense areas.	Hierarchies naturally emerge within a set territory as flows respond to contextual conditions in the course of optimizing their access—particularly in transitions from laminar to turbulent flow.	Vertical transfers of water are facilitated within forested patches either by ground recharge or from ground to air with trees acting as pumps moving water from wet to dry conditions. As in all energy flows, moisture gravitates toward equilibrium.	Balance in multi-scale design dictates that the time to move fast and long should roughly equal the time to move slow and short. Sheet or diffused flow is balanced with turbulent flow accommodated through channels.

Sponge City Gradient

These hybrid infrastructural solutions also offer a highly imagistic, resilient urban landscape foundational to achieving a holistic *watershed approach*.

The six water treatment technologies provide the building blocks for developing a citywide treatment landscape in the watershed approach. To slow, soak, and spread stormwater runoff, first enhance landscape biodiversity since ecological-based management solutions require healthy soils, plant communities, and riparian systems. This subsequently allows the treatment system to maximize water infiltration and eliminate peak flow runoffs damaging to both urban and ecosystem functioning. Runoff treatment systems should be engineered in distributed networks based on redundancy, high connectivity, and modularity to create a resilient urban landscape. This recalls Wendell Berry's adage in his book, *The Gift of Good Land,* that "a good solution in one pattern preserves the integrity of the pattern that contains it." The Sponge City Gradient and the Six Water Management and Treatment Technologies combined provide a city-building vocabulary and watershed approach for remedying water resource management problems.

A Plan that Works Incrementally

The Framework Plan operates evolutionarily through a set of retrofit types that are incremental, contextual, and *successional*. The Framework Plan is incremental, relying on participation from various interests—public, private, or a combination thereof—to develop projects as funding and opportunity permit. Projects can be implemented step-wise in small batches across various fronts in the urbanized area. Unlike the master plan which is totalizing and shows only a climax condition, the Framework Plan can be pioneered beginning with modest cumulative efforts that cohere from shared ecological design practices.

The Framework Plan is contextual, working through landscape architectural adaptations responsive to local ecologies and urban water problems. Soft engineering accounts for local soils, and vegetative and wildlife communities in place-based solutions that substitute for universal metrics and costly "over-engineered" outcomes driven by worst case scenarios. The goal is to deliver ecological services through installing sustainable soft infrastructure that also delivers ecological services. Soft engineering's use of *adaptive management* lessens long-term maintenance burdens associated with hard-engineered infrastructure.

The Framework Plan is successional, understanding that cities are not built at once and that pioneer stages of development are rudimentary as they minimize start-up costs. *The Framework Plan works initially through tactical demonstration projects*, which if approved after assessment, can be mainstreamed into future projects and policies. This way the city or project developer can evaluate new practices without committing permanently to an untested development and business model. Cities do not have to retool policies without the chance to pursue due diligence. Stakeholders in decision-making, including the city and the area's new watershed alliances (e.g., the Lake Conway-Point Remove Watershed Alliance), can collaborate as *learning communities* removing adversarial relationships so redolent in municipal planning processes. Without demonstration projects, conventional development ap-

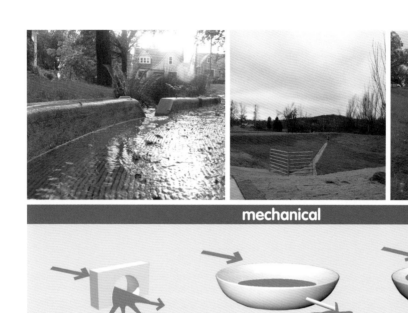

mechanical

slow ————————————————————————————→ s p

flow control: The regulation of stormwater runoff flow rates.

detention: The temporary storage of stormwater runoff in underground vaults, ponds, or depressed areas to allow for metered discharge that reduce peak flow rates.

retention: The storage of stormwater runoff on site to allow for sedimentation of suspended solids.

Water Treatmen

proaches will remain entrenched despite the existence of more value-added approaches. Conway's growth and governance successes suggest that it is prepared for the next development stage toward holistic and high-value outcomes.

Conclusion

Where the two networks meet—the city and water—can certainly be a source for many solutions to myriad development problems. The Framework Plan places Conway ahead of the curve in addressing the greatest ongoing challenge to planning: development of urban form in human-dominated ecosystems. More cities are tasking urban infrastructure with regeneration of dimin-

Source: *Low Impact Development: a design manual for urban areas*, UACDC

biological

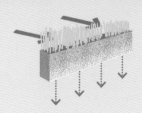
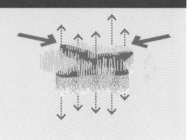

a d ————————————————————————→ **soak**

filtration: The seques-
tration of sediment
from stormwater run-
off through a porous
media such as sand,
a fibrous root system,
or a man-made filter.

infiltration: The
vertical movement
of stormwater runoff
through soil, recharg-
ing groundwater.

treatment: Processes
that utilize phytore-
mediation or bacterial
colonies to metabo-
lize contaminants in
stormwater runoff.

Technologies

ished ecosystems to support livable communities. Besides solving for water
management problems like flooding, the collateral benefits of implementing
the plan include greater livability, sustained economic development, improved
community resilience to disruption and shocks, and exemplary beauty in the
civic realm that creates enduring value and symbolism.

Context
Characterization

Arkansas has 58 watersheds of which 10 have been designated as priority watersheds due to *nonpoint source pollution*, including the Lake Conway-Point Remove Watershed. LCPRW is without a USEPA approved management plan, limiting the area's access to funding for implementing urban watershed improvements. The Little Creek-Palarm Creek sub-watershed—the focus of this Framework Plan—drains over half of the City of Conway, with Lake Conway, the state's largest game and fish lake, as the receiving water body. Rapid urban growth without proper water management planning is resulting in watershed dysfunction and lake impairment. Recent studies indicate significant increases in sedimentation, phosphorus and organic matter in Lake Conway. Extreme flooding events in 2008, 2009, and 2011 appear to have driven these increases. Stone Dam Creek and Palarm Creek exhibit the highest average sedimentation rates. Erosion and sedimentation are significant problems in the Little Creek-Palarm Creek corridors and a majority of the watershed's urbanized area lacks the riparian cover recommended by the National Resources Conservation Service.

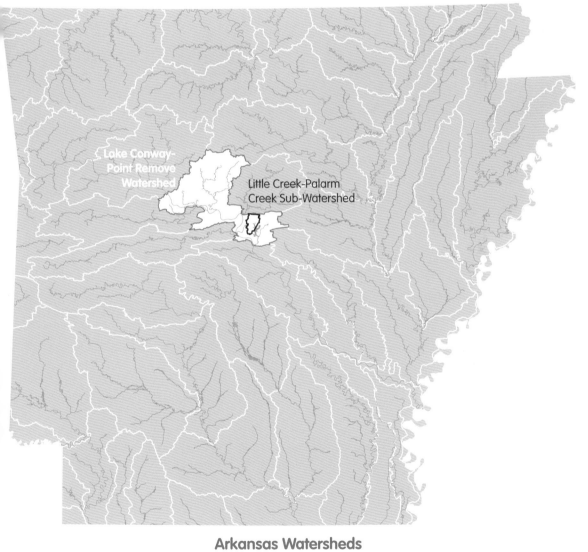

Lake Conway-
Point Remove
Watershed

Little Creek-Palarm
Creek Sub-Watershed

Arkansas Watersheds

0   25   50 miles

Context Characterization: Lake Conway-Point Remove Watershed

Covering over a 1,144 square mile area (HUC 11110203), the population in this watershed totals 131,391 based on the 2010 U.S. Census.

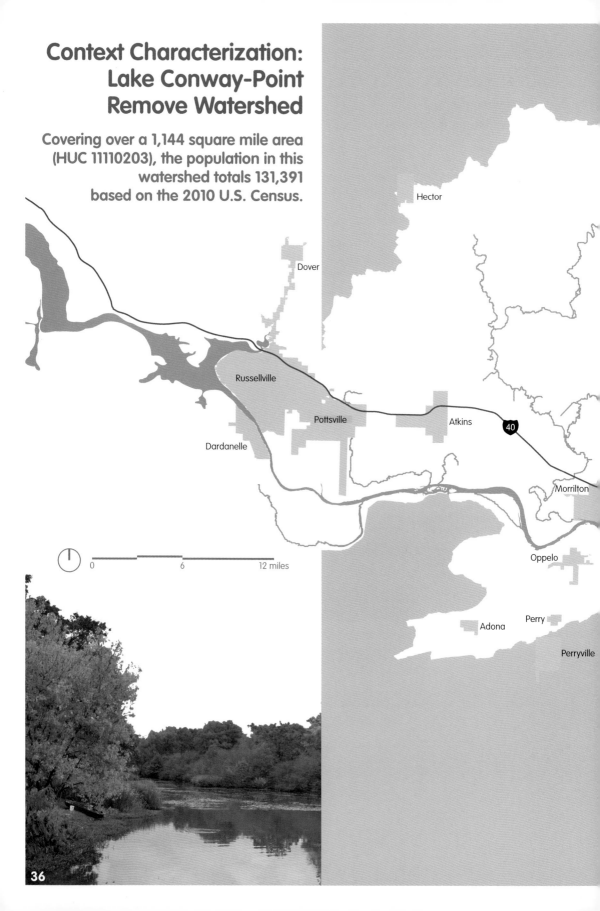

Hector

Dover

Russellville

Pottsville

Atkins

40

Dardanelle

Morrilton

0   6   12 miles

Oppelo

Perry

Adona

Perryville

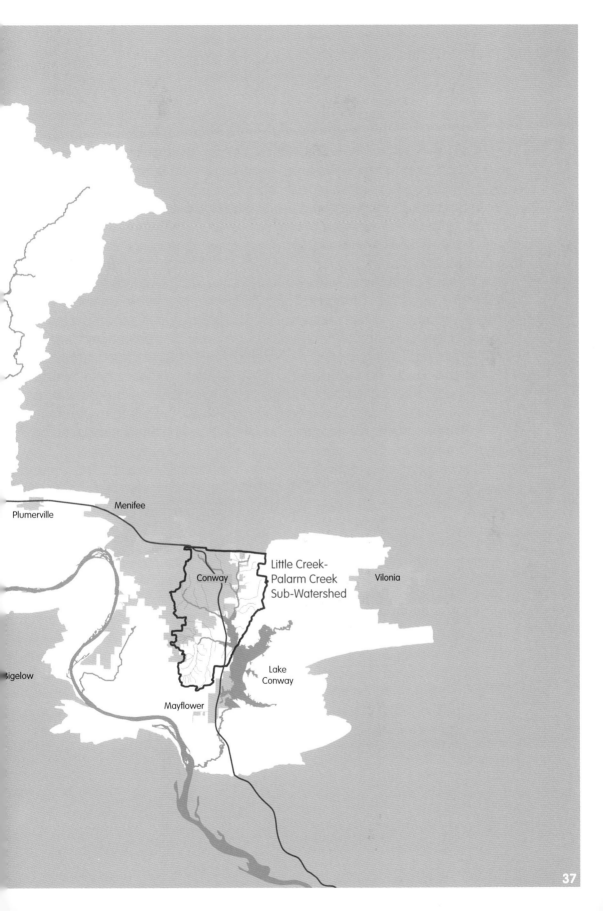

Plumerville

Menifee

Conway

Little Creek-
Palarm Creek
Sub-Watershed

Vilonia

Bigelow

Lake
Conway

Mayflower

Context Characterization: Ecoregions of Arkansas

The Lake Conway-Point Remove Watershed lies in the interface of four distinct Level IV ecoregions, Arkansas Valley Hills, Scattered High Ridges, Arkansas Valley Plains, and the Fourche Mountains with each region having distinct soil types, topography and biota. The majority of the watershed lies within the Arkansas Valley with hills and plains comprising the greatest portion. Watershed vegetation types are composed of oak-hickory-pine forest in the hills and savanna-prairie in the plains.

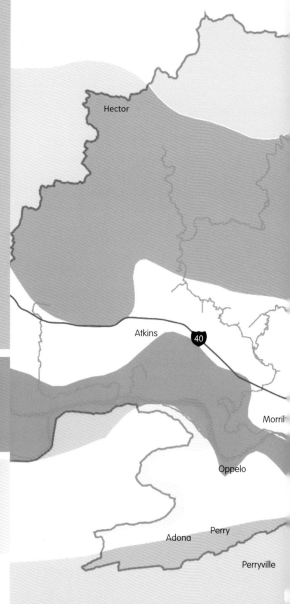

Hector

Atkins

40

Morril

Oppelo

Adona   Perry

Perryville

Arkansas Valley Hills

Scattered High Ridges

Arkansas Valley Plains

Fourche Mountains

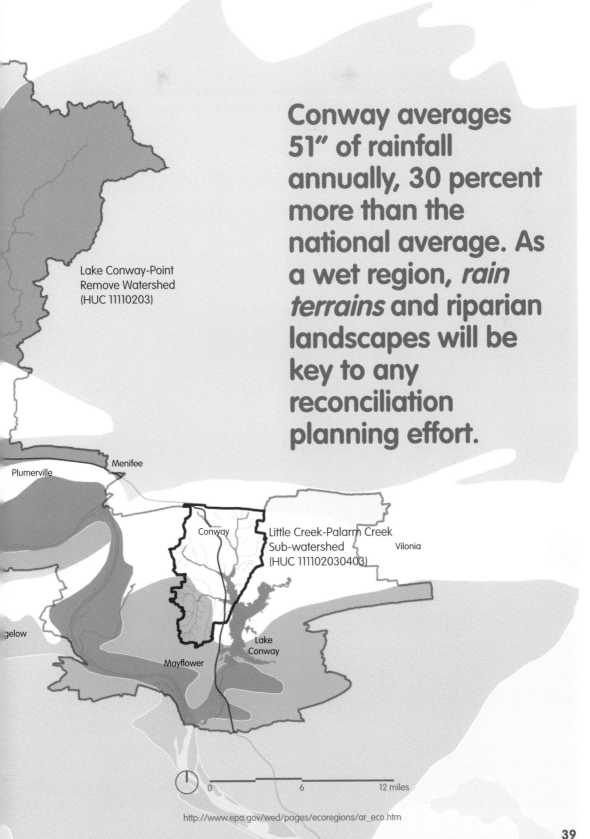

Lake Conway-Point Remove Watershed (HUC 11110203)

Conway averages 51" of rainfall annually, 30 percent more than the national average. As a wet region, *rain terrains* and riparian landscapes will be key to any reconciliation planning effort.

Plumerville

Menifee

Conway

Little Creek-Palarm Creek Sub-watershed (HUC 111102030403)

Vilonia

gelow

Mayflower

Lake Conway

0   6   12 miles

http://www.epa.gov/wed/pages/ecoregions/ar_eco.htm

Context Characterization: Urban Impacts

Since the first hour of urban stormwater runoff can have a pollution index greater than that of raw sewage, stormwater treatment becomes imperative because everything upstream within the sub-watershed eventually makes its way into Lake Conway.

The urbanized portions of the City of Conway with the greatest impervious surface area drain into the lake. Known as nonpoint source pollution, surface level pollutants generated by diffused human activities are concentrated and transported by stormwater runoff into local water bodies since there is no municipal underground storm sewer system.

Nonpoint source pollution can be natural or human-made pollutants including synthetic fertilizers, herbicides, and insecticides from urban and agricultural lands; oil, grease, metals and coolants from automobiles; toxic chemicals from road construction, industrial sites, and energy production; sediment from construction sites, agricultural and forested land and eroding stream banks; and bacteria and nutrient loading from livestock, pets, and failing septic and sewer treatment systems.

Hendrix College

Downtown
Conway

UCA
Campus

County
Fairgrounds

Little Creek

Stone Dam Creek

Lake Conway

Little Creek-Palarm Creek Sub-watershed
HUC 111102030403

0   1.5   3 miles

Context Characterization: Urban Tree Canopy

Forested areas in Conway's ecoregion with a high *leaf area index* can intercept up to 35 percent of rainfall before it hits the ground according to foresters. High LAI can result in significant mitigation of urban stormwater impacts, particularly in areas with high levels of impervious surface.

The sub-watershed has good tree coverage to the south and in the historic neighborhoods. However, tree coverage is inadequate in the suburbs and in areas where the city is growing. The forested plateau south of Conway is beginning to show signs of deforestation due to residential development and conversion to pasture land and mining. The loss of vegetative cover coupled with steep topography is a potential threat for increased sedimentation and lake flooding, already chronic problems.

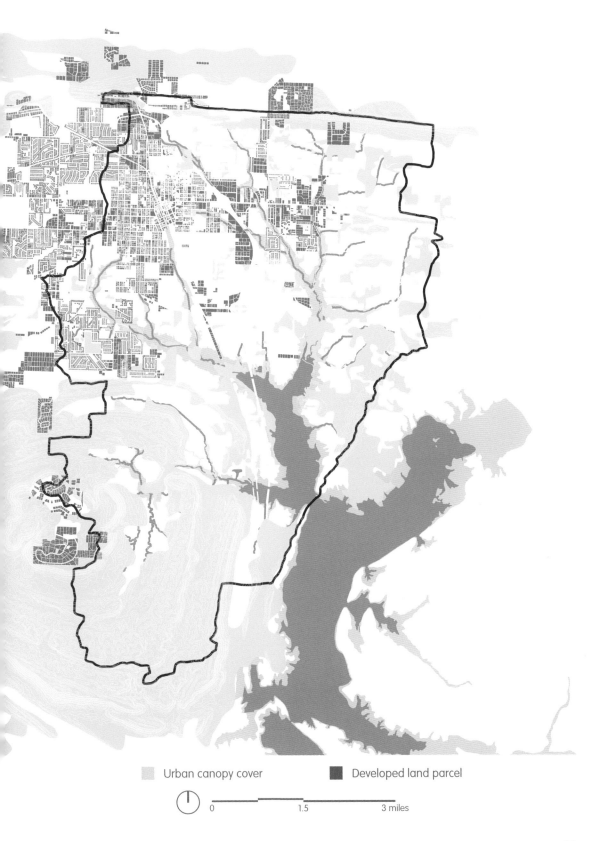

Urban canopy cover   Developed land parcel

0   1.5   3 miles

Context Characterization: Growth Profile

Since more than a third of the City's built environment projected to exist by 2030 has not yet been built, now is the time to implement a green infrastructure plan that leverages ecological and economic returns in future growth.

Conway's population is projected to grow by more than 25,000 to 88,000 by 2030. This entails more than 10,000 new dwelling units covering more than 3,400 acres if current density trends of three units per acre persist. This does not factor in the infrastructure or the non-residential land use footprint which will add considerably more impervious surface area. Growth can be a liability or an asset, dependent upon the City's use of planning as a resource to develop the type of place it aims to be.

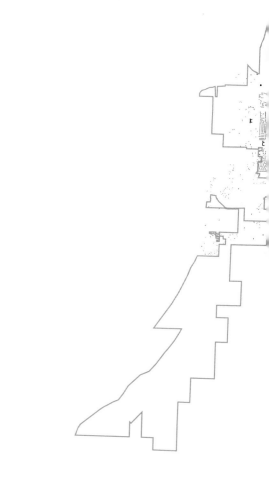

Conway, Arkansas
38,528 acres (population 62,596)

0   1.5   3 miles

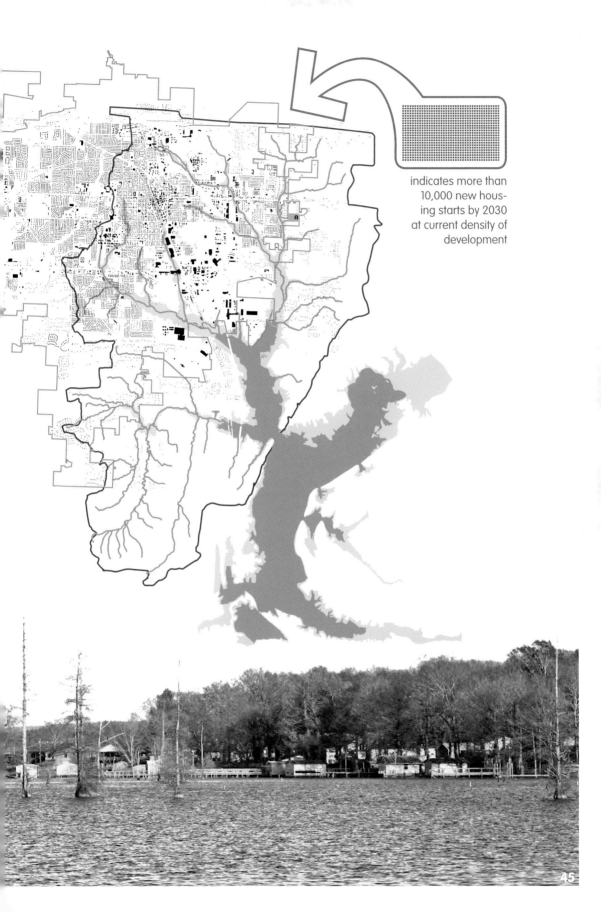

indicates more than
10,000 new hous-
ing starts by 2030
at current density of
development

Context Characterization: Asphalt Coverage

Research shows that more than 10 percent coverage of surface area with impervious surfaces from roofs, parking lots, and roads can lead to regional watershed damage, while more than 30 percent coverage can lead to irreversible watershed destruction.

Many of the parking lots shown are, by design and policy, oversized for their programmatic needs. They were constructed in a time when the need for ecologically-based management of stormwater runoff was not well understood, especially the direct discharge of untreated urban runoff into local streams. These parking lots are great opportunities for green infrastructure retrofits that effectively manage stormwater runoff while creating great places and branding opportunities for commercial land uses.

0   1.5   3 miles

Context Characterization: Ecological Stressors

The City's robust industrial legacy has left behind brownfield sites with large impervious surface areas and/or areas of highly compacted soil that discharge urban runoff directly into urban streams. Area soil structure is not conducive to deep infiltration of stormwater, compounding problems in surface water conveyance.

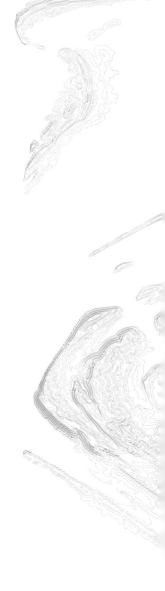

structures built on top of stream

loss of riparian landscape

stream channelization

large impervious tarmac

stream inputs from industry + construction

Soil Quality

Moderate Infiltration; silt loam/loam

Low Infiltration; sandy clay loam

No Infiltration; clay loam/silty clay/clay

● Ecological stressor

0   1.5   3 miles

re-inventing Conway

Infrastructure for the 21st century city simply will have to do more work. The City's growth and governance successes suggest that it is prepared for the next development stage toward holistic and high-value outcomes.

so then let's examine the present challenges...

wrong kind of land and stream interface

Direct discharge of polluted stormwater runoff into streams was a common practice before improved understanding of environmental and biological processes. The best practice is to manage and retain water on-site, or treat urban runoff before its release into a water body…remember, the first flush can have a pollution index far higher than that of raw sewage.

Problemscape

A map of the myriad manifestations of nonpoint source pollution, and their expressions in stream dysfunction across the sub-watershed, forms the starting point for an Urban Watershed Framework Plan. While the human activities indicated are not intrinsically defective, but rather essential to our economies, their unregulated outputs become "negative externalities"—i.e., the public's problems and cost burdens—when not reconciled with watershed functioning. A holistic approach to watershed management is within easy grasp.

Sedimentation   Parking + Brownfields

Impervious Urban Area   Agriculture

Nutrient + Chemical Loading   Septic Tank + Lake Flooding + Concrete Walls

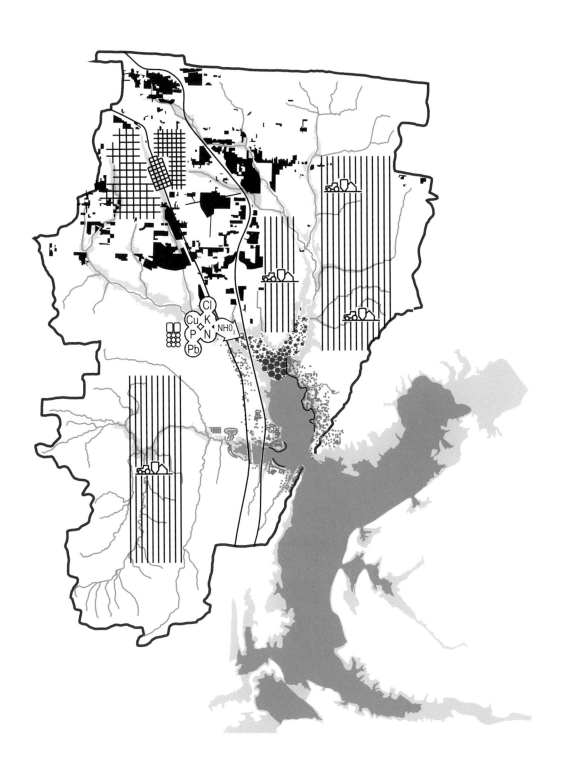

Problemscape: Five Riparian Corridors

The watershed is only as healthy as its constituent streams and the respective characteristics of the ecoregions in which they originate. Each of the five riparian corridors shaping the Little Creek-Palarm Creek sub-watershed reside in human-dominated ecosystems.

These five riparian corridors bear the imprints of urbanization and/or intensive agriculture, much of it developed before widespread understanding of the value of watershed integrity. While streams in this sub-watershed have traditionally been treated as stormwater detention and conveyance facilities—leading to urban stream syndrome—the good news is that these dated practices are easy to correct leading to multiplier benefits in watershed health and urban livability. This entails restoration of necessary corridor components like floodplains, vegetated banks, and sinuosity in stream geometries. Indeed, fixing the problems gives rise to a unique urban brandscape otherwise elusive in conventional planning processes.

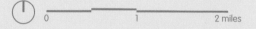

0   1   2 miles

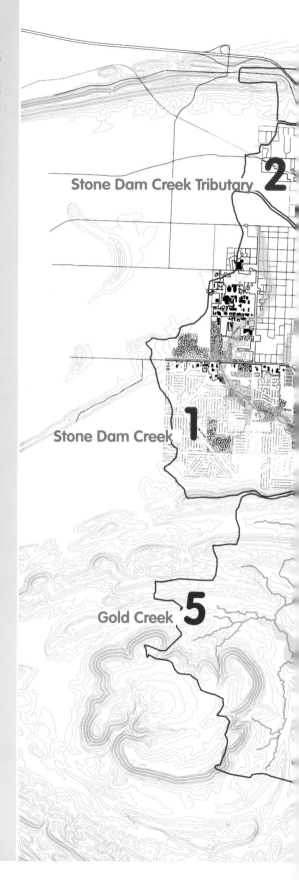

Stone Dam Creek Tributary **2**

Stone Dam Creek **1**

Gold Creek **5**

3 Little Creek

4 Little Creek Tributary

Lake Conway

1 Stone Dam Creek Problemscape

Flowing through the City's first-ring suburbs, this riparian corridor receives sheet flows from invasive turf lawns supplemented by industrial herbicides, pesticides, and fertilizers, as well as nonpoint source inputs from campus parking lots and vacated industrial parcels.

Unprotected headwaters ❶
Impervious pavement adjacent to the stream, and piping and channelization of the stream's headwaters increase runoff velocity and volume which diminishes aquatic habitat downstream.

Loss of riparian vegetation ❷
Livestock grazing and trampling increases sedimentation and accelerates pollutant flows into the stream.

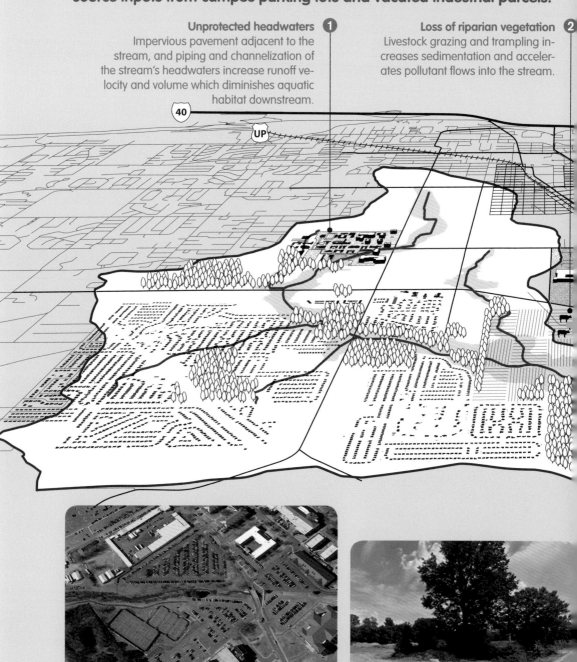

Campus development and parking within floodplain

Loss of riparian edge

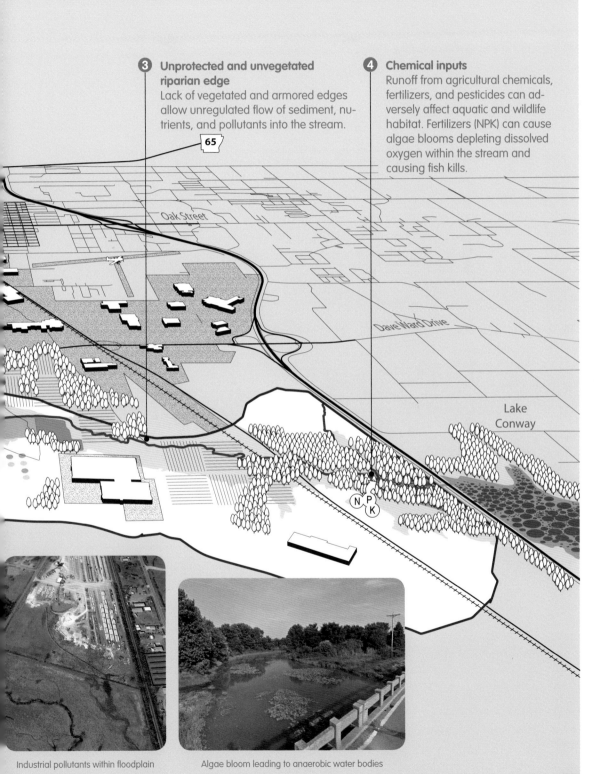

3 **Unprotected and unvegetated riparian edge**
Lack of vegetated and armored edges allow unregulated flow of sediment, nutrients, and pollutants into the stream.

65

4 **Chemical inputs**
Runoff from agricultural chemicals, fertilizers, and pesticides can adversely affect aquatic and wildlife habitat. Fertilizers (NPK) can cause algae blooms depleting dissolved oxygen within the stream and causing fish kills.

Oak Street

Dave Ward Drive

Lake Conway

N P K

Industrial pollutants within floodplain

Algae bloom leading to anaerobic water bodies

2 Stone Dam Creek Tributary Problemscape

Flowing through downtown and the industrial district along the railroad—and piped underneath industrial structures—this riparian corridor is managed through channelization and piping that exacerbate downstream problems.

Unprotected headwaters ❶
Headwater shortcomings compound physical, biological and chemical aquatic health downstream.

❷ Channelization and piping
Hard-engineered solutions eliminate the self-correcting capacity intrinsic to the stream's natural ecology.

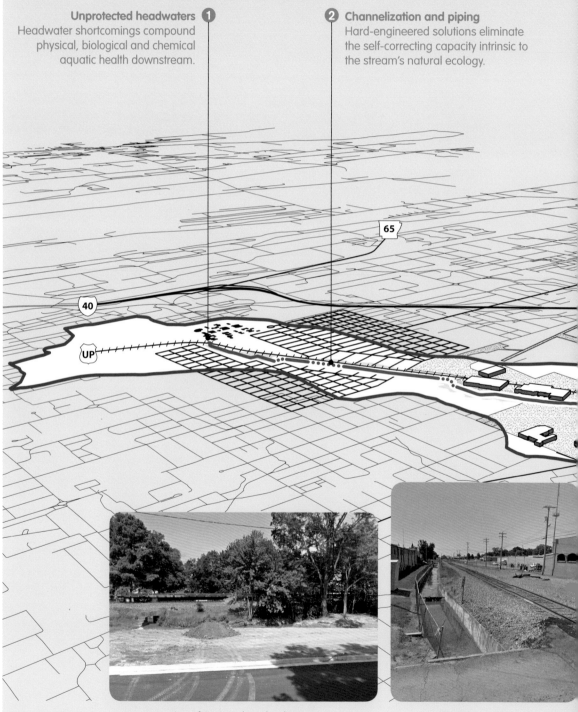

Loss of riparian edge at headwaters

Channelization of stream

③ Industrial development over stream
Piped streams increase threats from chemical pollutants entering surface waters as well as decrease water retention time, creating velocity and flow problems further downstream.

④ Chemical inputs
Runoff from agricultural chemicals, fertilizers, and pesticides can adversely affect aquatic and wildlife habitat. Fertilizers (NPK) can cause algae blooms depleting dissolved oxygen within the stream and causing fish kills.

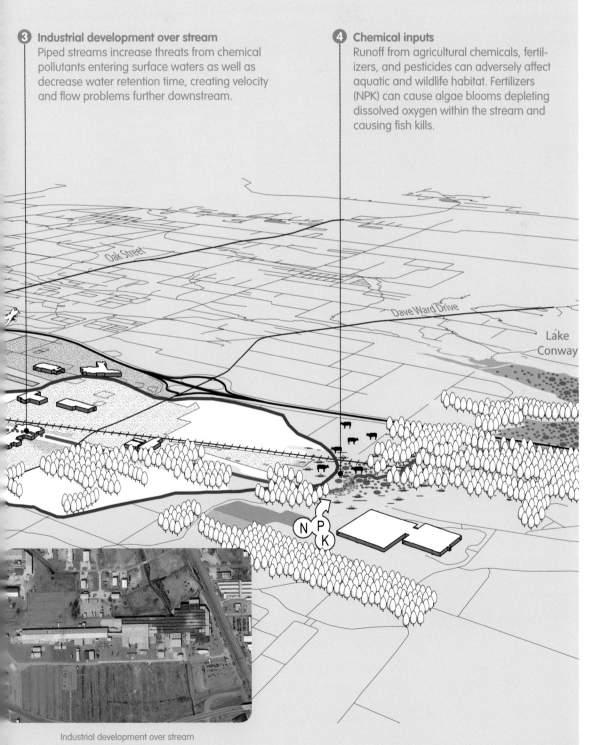

Industrial development over stream

3 Little Creek Problemscape

Flowing through suburban contexts populated with auto-oriented commercial centers, large parking lots and scrap operations, this riparian corridor receives peak storm inputs with minimal floodplain and vegetation to mitigate excessive flow energy and sedimentation.

Expanse of impervious paving along stream ❶
Impervious surfaces prevent rainwater infiltration and groundwater recharge while increasing the velocity and flow of stormwater runoff.

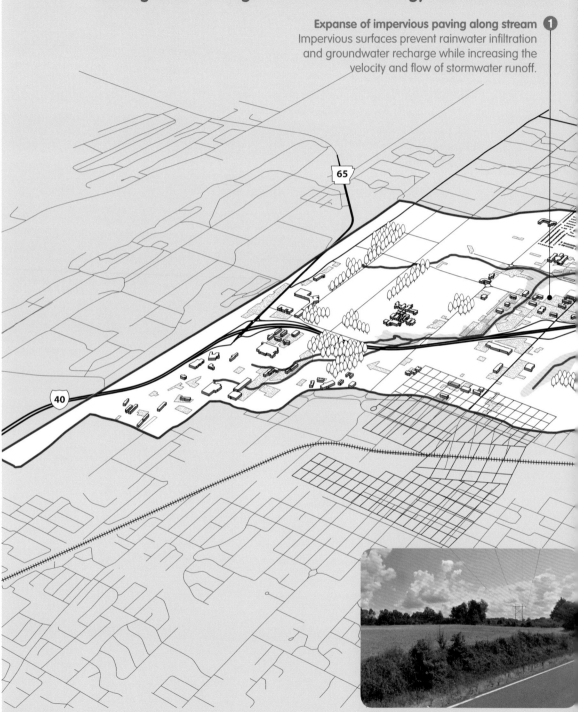

Loss of cover crop to retain top soil

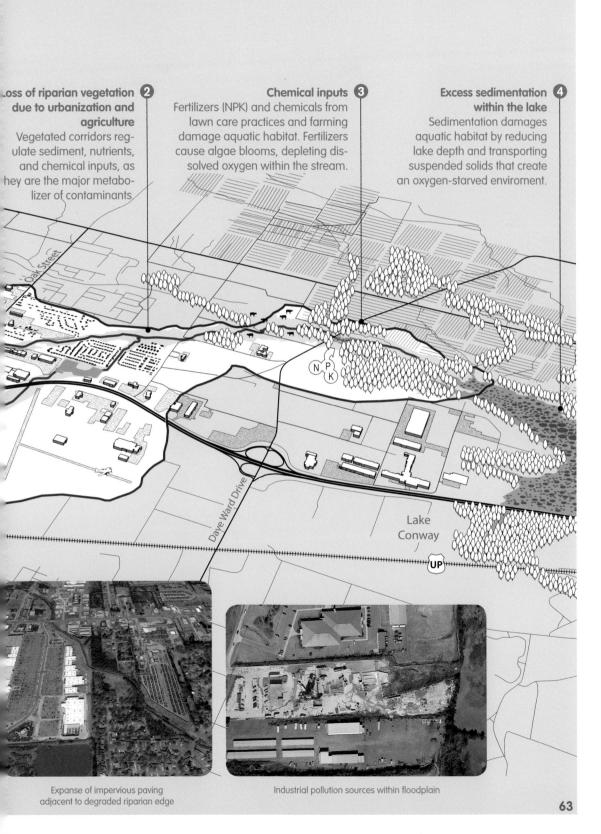

Loss of riparian vegetation ❷
due to urbanization and
agriculture
Vegetated corridors reg-
ulate sediment, nutrients,
and chemical inputs, as
they are the major metabo-
lizer of contaminants.

Chemical inputs ❸
Fertilizers (NPK) and chemicals from
lawn care practices and farming
damage aquatic habitat. Fertilizers
cause algae blooms, depleting dissolved oxygen within the stream.

Excess sedimentation ❹
within the lake
Sedimentation damages
aquatic habitat by reducing
lake depth and transporting
suspended solids that create
an oxygen-starved enviroment.

Oak Street

Dave Ward Drive

Lake
Conway

Expanse of impervious paving
adjacent to degraded riparian edge

Industrial pollution sources within floodplain

63

4 Little Creek Tributary Problemscape

Flowing through primarily agricultural land uses and low-density residential development, this riparian corridor suffers from loss of functioning riparian edges due to land use encroachments on the stream system.

Loss of floodplain by residential and **1**
agricultural encroachment
Floodplains deliver a high rate of ecological services and are usually the first riparian elements eliminated by encroaching development.

Livestock trampled and grazed riparian vegetation

Loss of riparian edge

Agricultural chemical inputs ❷
Runoff from agricultural chemicals can adversely affect aquatic and wildlife habitat. Fertilizers (NPK) can cause algae blooms depleting dissolved oxygen within the stream. Both fertilizers and pesticides can cause fish kills.

❸ **Livestock adjacent to stream**
Results in animal waste migration to the stream and destruction of the riparian edge from grazing and trampling.

Lake Conway

Dave Ward Drive

Loss of vegetation within bioswales

5 Gold Creek Problemscape

Flowing down a primarily forested hilltop, this riparian corridor has experienced encroachment from agricultural and residential land uses the stream system.

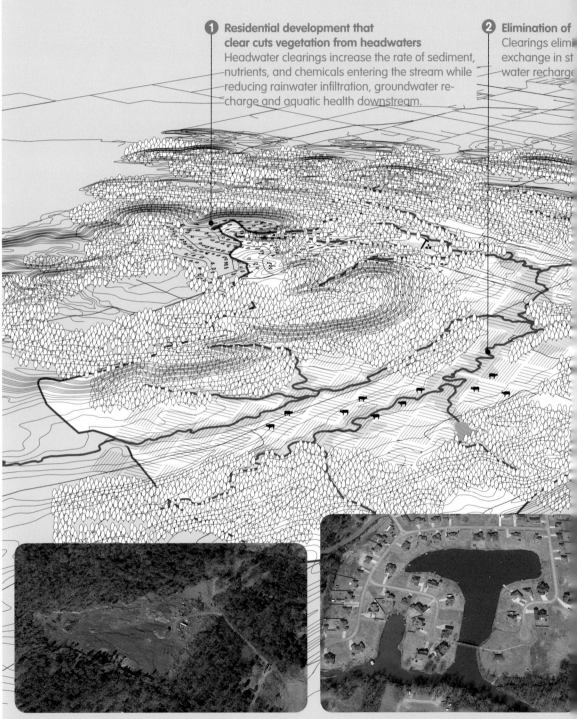

1 Residential development that clear cuts vegetation from headwaters
Headwater clearings increase the rate of sediment, nutrients, and chemicals entering the stream while reducing rainwater infiltration, groundwater recharge and aquatic health downstream.

2 Elimination of
Clearings elimi
exchange in st
water recharge

Mining within watershed threatens water quality due to erosion and pollutants

Loss of riparian edge causes direct nutrient and chemical input from fertilizers and pesticides

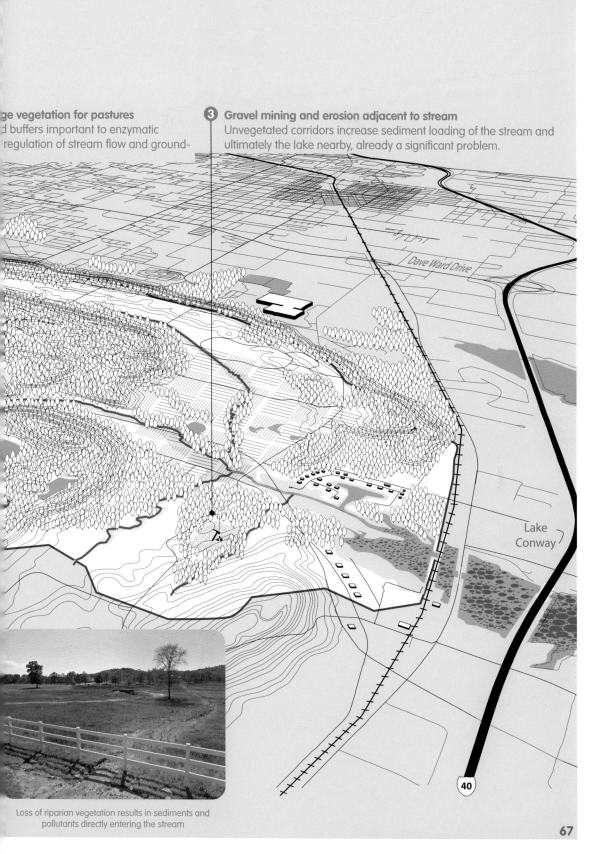

ge vegetation for pastures
d buffers important to enzymatic
 regulation of stream flow and ground-

3 Gravel mining and erosion adjacent to stream
Unvegetated corridors increase sediment loading of the stream and
ultimately the lake nearby, already a significant problem.

Dave Ward Drive

Lake
Conway

40

Loss of riparian vegetation results in sediments and
pollutants directly entering the stream

why not the best of both worlds ?

Cities, like all flow systems, tend to evolve ever more efficient configurations inclined to privilege the specialized currents that pass through them—cars, people, and goods. Likewise, the watershed is a flow network modeled by biological processes. Where the city and the watershed meet presents the greatest opportunities for hybrid solutions reconciling the demands in each.

...from the challenges, let's move to planning approaches that reconcile city and water...

Urban Watershed Framework Plan

How can city form fix the watershed? Because the Framework Plan should not be prescriptive, the plan is structured around likely interface possibilities within each of the four levels of interaction between city and water—see Sponge City Gradient (in Executive Summary). The plan is modular, facilitating incremental implementation by various stakeholders across the sub-watershed, in the interest of eventually building a holistic framework. The challenge for stakeholders involves matching land use opportunities with the right Framework Plan strategies responsive to pixilated, nested, clustered, or connected interfaces between city and water. Every part of the urbanized area, including downtown, has a role to play in the creation of a green cityscape with good water quality and healthy watershed functioning.

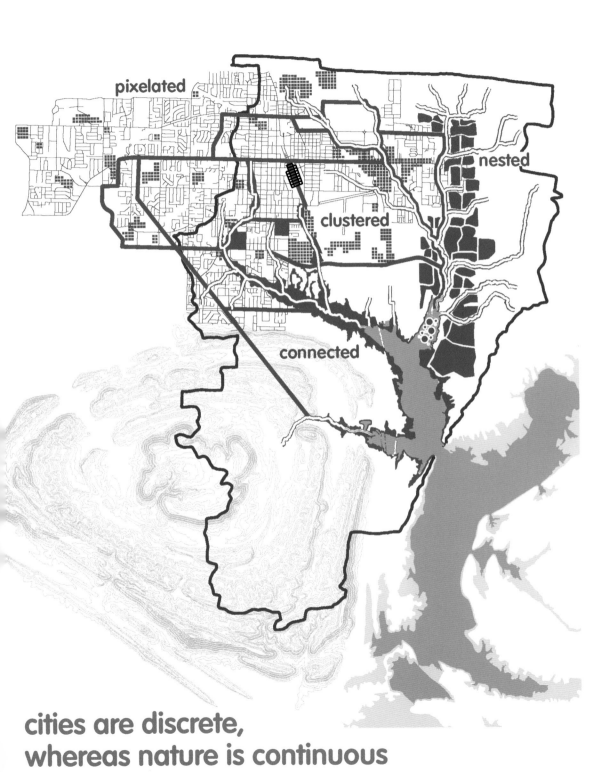

pixelated

nested

clustered

connected

**cities are discrete,
whereas nature is continuous**

Framework Plan: Adaptive Infrastructure

Lake Restoration ❶
Enhancement of lake ecology requires tactical operations to normalize sediment and water flows at the edge, on the surface, and within the lake.

Green Streets and Parks ❷
Streets and parks can be designed to deliver ecological services through alternative right-of-way configurations and landscape technologies embedded in street design. These strategies can be scaled to various types of public space.

Parking Gardens ❸
Employing functional water treatment landscapes, parking lots can be designed to metabolize their own pollution generated by stormwater runoff and hydrocarbons from automobiles.

Urban Eco-Farm ❹
As generators of nutrient overloads discharged to streams, farms can be designed to upcycle their outputs, eliminating the concept of waste in favor of higher economic returns and energy efficiencies.

Conservation Development ❺
Conservation development is premised on clustered patterns of housing, infrastructure, and landscape to create unique neighborhoods of high vitality and interest, assembled from commonplace neighborhood components.

City Greenway ❻
Incorporating both streams and street networks, greenway segments—or loops—form a third flow system delivering urban and ecological services scaled to neighborhoods.

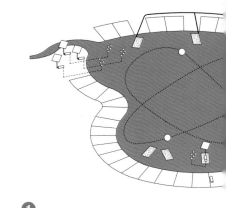

❶

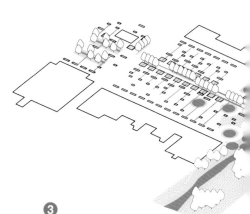

❸

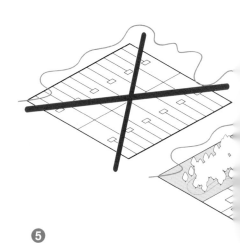

❺

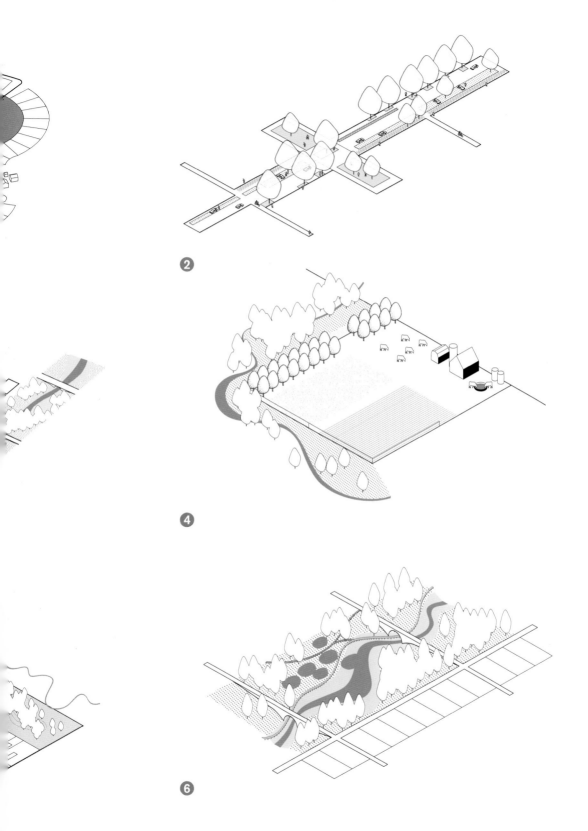

2

4

6

let's begin exploration of the plan by re-imagining lake Conway

1990

2015

2018

Lake Restoration

Lakes and reservoirs are quasi-closed energy systems requiring a continual influx of nutrients. However, Lake Conway has been excessively enriched with sediments and nutrients due to human activities and requires ecologically-based interventions to reclaim a more balanced relationship with its headwaters.

Floating Wetland Islands

Retrofitted Septic Tanks

Revegetated Edge

Surface Aerators/Solar Harvesters

Dredging

Restored Wetlands

Lake Restoration

Restore lake edges and wetlands since they act as "kidneys" to regulate flow energy and mitigate flooding impacts, which in turn enhance the lake's cultural and recreational environment.

Then

Surface Operations

To return dissolved oxygen to the lake, aerate the water through solar-powered devices, and remove aquatic weeds through an automated plant harvester. Install floating bio-mats, housing *phytoremediation* plant guilds, to filter excess nutrients.

Lake Edge Operations

Restore lake edge through grass and forest buffers as biofilters, including the use of natural erosion barriers or "biosausages" for subsurface composting. Develop a septic management plan, including inspection and retrofit of aging septic systems, and consider pump systems to replace leach fields close to the waterfront.

40

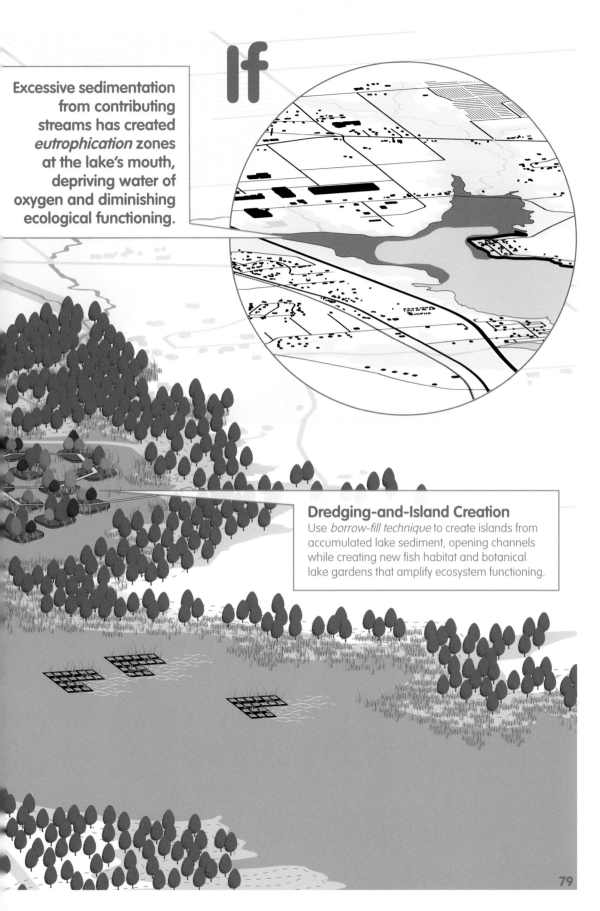

If

Excessive sedimentation from contributing streams has created *eutrophication* zones at the lake's mouth, depriving water of oxygen and diminishing ecological functioning.

Dredging-and-Island Creation

Use *borrow-fill technique* to create islands from accumulated lake sediment, opening channels while creating new fish habitat and botanical lake gardens that amplify ecosystem functioning.

Lake Restoration

Restored Riparian Corridor ❶
Improve riparian stream buffers to slow and filter stormwater runoff.

Dredging + Wetland Island Formations ❷
Form islands from selective dredging and stockpiling lake bottom sediment.

Restored Wetland Habitat ❸
Improve wetlands to filter, purify, and store water.

Retrofitted Septic Tanks ❹
Incent remediation of aging septic systems.

Solar Weed Harvester Aquabot ❺
Employ aquabots to remove excessive or invasive lake vegetation, "underwater lawn mowers."

Floating Bio-Mats ❻
Use treatment facilities that provide aquatic, bird, and animal habitat with microbial communities that metabolize excess nutrients.

Solar Aeration Aquabot ❼
Use aquabots that increase oxygenation in water, enhancing aquatic habitat.

Removal of Concrete Walls ❽
Reestablish the natural stream bank edges and ecological functioning.

Community Waste Water Treatment Plant ❾
Consider the role of small Community Centralized Cluster systems for collective septic services.

Native Mussels ❿
Introduce these endangered nutrient filters into water bodies to reduce harmful bacteria, especially E. coli, and to consume algae.

0   .25   .5 miles

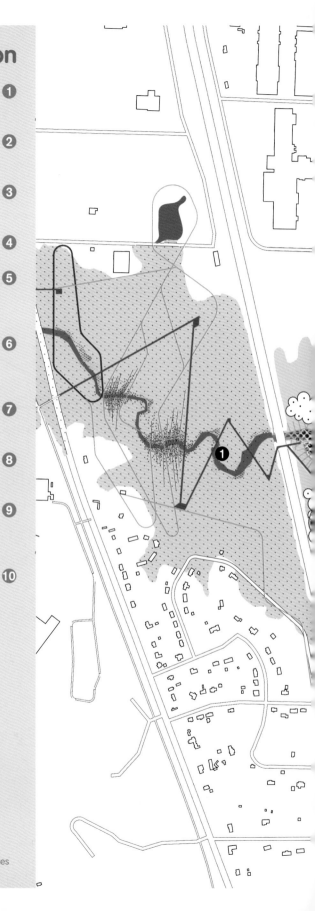

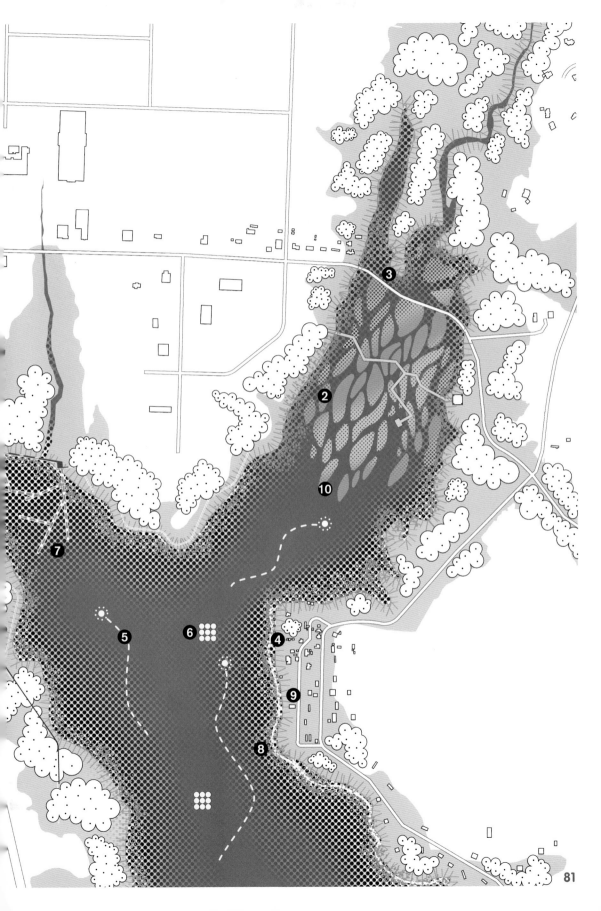

Lake Restoration Tools

Solar Weed Harvester Aquabot
The harvester gathers floating debris and algae, while functioning as an underwater lawnmower uprooting, mulching, and transporting lake bottom vegetation for removal. This curbs the need for spraying herbicides within the lake. The self-automated stainless steel harvester floats like a boat and is propelled by a paddle wheel and solar powered engine with the capability of operating in as low as 12" of water.

Solar Aeration Aquabot
The "Solar Bee" is a solar powered aerator that mixes oxygen-rich water from the top of the lake with oxygen-depleted water from the bottom of the lake. A system of paddles both mixes water and propels the device around the lake. The Solar Bee also helps control lake odor.

Floating Bio-Mat
The mat is a hydroponic system that functions as a concentrated wetland habitat. It is composed of natural coir (coconut husk fiber) and a peat matrix planted with native wetland vegetation. Emergent vegetation serves as wildlife habitat for birds, insects, and amphibians while providing fish habitat supported by a rich layer of bio-film, and micro-organism colonies in association with plant roots below. Microbes and roots metabolize nutrients and chemical pollutants. These mats are suitable for phytoremediation application uses in streams, wetlands, and lake environments.

Solar Weed Harvester Aquabot

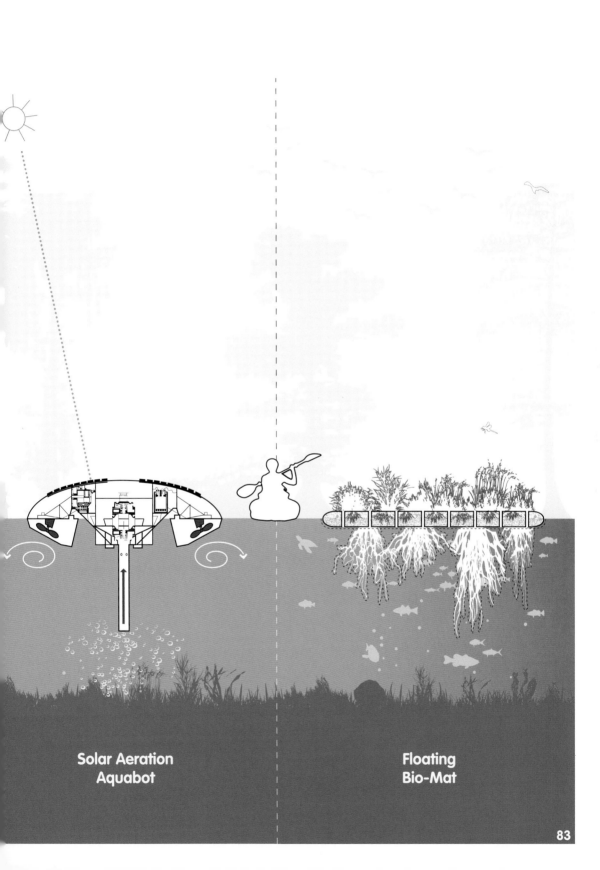

Solar Aeration
Aquabot

Floating
Bio-Mat

The 17 Ecosystem Services

Ecosystem services are the flow of energy, materials, and information from natural systems that support human life. The 2006 *Millennium Ecosystem Assessment* distinguishes four categories of ecosystem services— **provisioning, regulating, supporting,** and **cultural**. Supporting services underpin the services delivered in the other three categories. Since the quality of ecosystem services is tied to place and ecoregion functioning, it is imperative that urbanization processes ensure watershed integrity by enhancing ecosystem services.

Provisioning Services describe the material or energy production from ecosystems, including food, water, and other essential resources.
- food production
- raw material production
- water supply

Regulating Services describe the regulatory functions in maintaining healthy water, air, and soil as essential life support systems, including flood, climate, and disease control.
- atmosphere regulation
- climate regulation
- disturbance regulation
- water regulation
- erosion control
- species control
- waste treatment

Supporting Services describe the functions necessary for the production of all other ecosystem services.
- refugia
- genetic resources
- pollination
- soil formation
- nutrient cycling

Cultural Services indicate a 'reference function' that supports human health, well being, and livability, as well as connection to place.
- recreation
- cultural enrichment

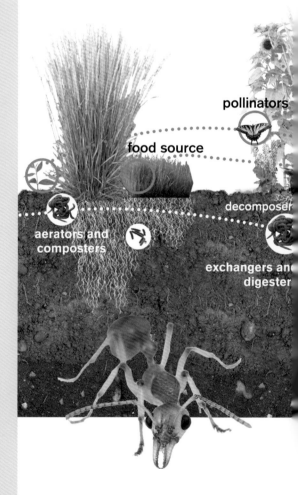

pollinators

food source

decomposer

aerators and composters

exchangers and digester

...a few thoughts on the formative role of ecosystem services in growing a city...

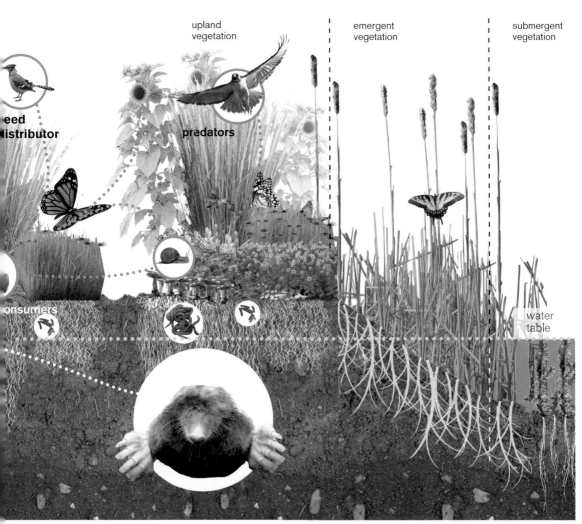

upland vegetation

emergent vegetation

submergent vegetation

eed istributor

predators

onsumers

water table

Source: *Low Impact Development: a design manual for urban areas*, UACDC

Lake Restoration:
Island Creation

Solar Lake Vegetation Harvester provides species control **regulating service** by removing algae, invasive or excessive *benthic* vegetation, curbing the need for spraying herbicides within the lake. Harvesting vegetation reduces excessive nutrient loads to improve water quality.

Solar Aeration Aquabot provides a water quality **regulating service** by balancing dissolved oxygen in low-flow water bodies, preventing build up of algae-dominant communities that eliminate aquatic life.

Floating Bio-Mats

provide the **regulating services** of a wetland, including water treatment, as microbial communities concentrated in mat habitats—akin to reefs—metabolize chemicals and filter suspended solids.

Lake Borrow-Fill Islands

are made from dredged nutrient-rich lake sediment to increase water clarity, providing a water quality **regulating service**, and a **supporting service** through addition of wildlife habitat and aquatic spawning areas. Reeds and grasses provide essential nesting areas.

Reintroduction of Endangered Mussels

like the Rabbitsfoot Mussel, to clean water by metabolizing harmful bacteria—especially E. coli, an indicator of fecal contamination—a critical **regulating service,** while providing the **supporting service** of restoring endangered species.

let's shift exploration of the plan to downtown— where ecology and economy intersect

More cities are tasking urban infrastructure with regeneration of diminished ecosystems to support livable communities. Besides solving for urban water management problems like flooding, the collateral benefits of implementing the Framework Plan include greater livability, sustained economic development, improved community resilience to disruption and shocks, and exemplary beauty in the civic realm that creates enduring value and symbolism.

Downtown Conway

Green Streets and Parks

2

All public right-of-ways and open spaces should offer water management functions as part of their public utility. As in all "great streets," non-traffic services related to ecological and social functioning can be reclaimed to make great places.

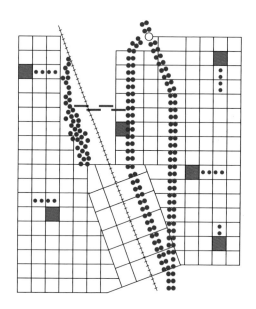

Downtown Green Loop	◗
Shared Green Street	‒ ‒
Green Alley	● ● ●
Neighborhood Parks	◼

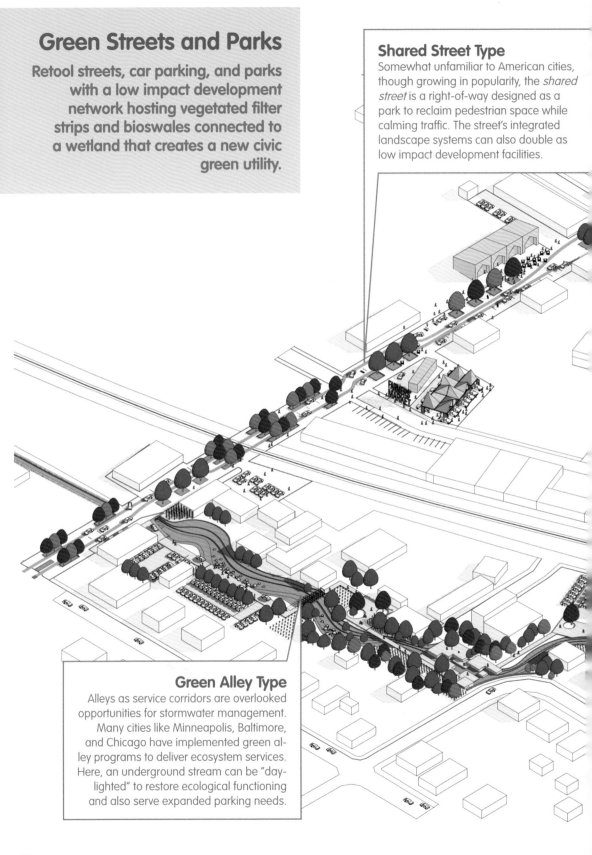

Green Streets and Parks

Retool streets, car parking, and parks with a low impact development network hosting vegetated filter strips and bioswales connected to a wetland that creates a new civic green utility.

Shared Street Type

Somewhat unfamiliar to American cities, though growing in popularity, the *shared street* is a right-of-way designed as a park to reclaim pedestrian space while calming traffic. The street's integrated landscape systems can also double as low impact development facilities.

Green Alley Type

Alleys as service corridors are overlooked opportunities for stormwater management. Many cities like Minneapolis, Baltimore, and Chicago have implemented green alley programs to deliver ecosystem services. Here, an underground stream can be "daylighted" to restore ecological functioning and also serve expanded parking needs.

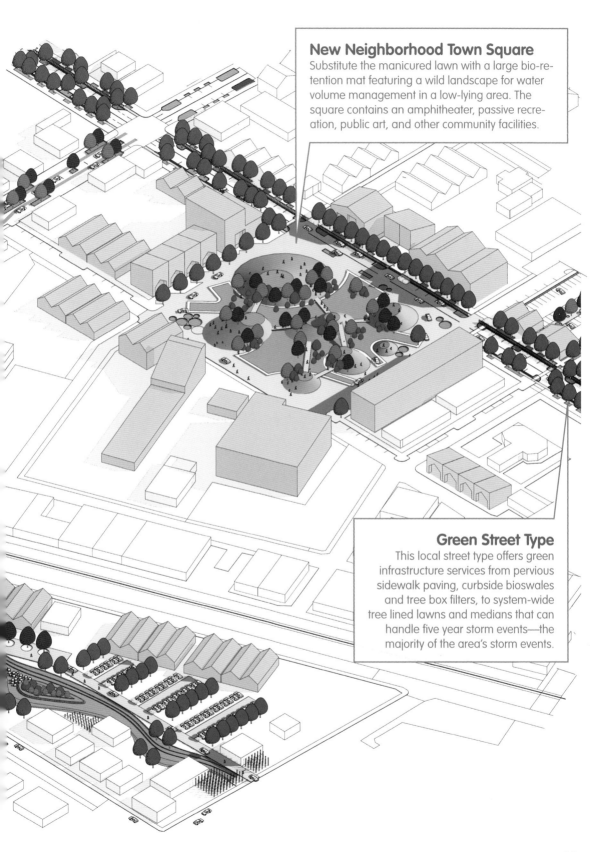

New Neighborhood Town Square
Substitute the manicured lawn with a large bio-retention mat featuring a wild landscape for water volume management in a low-lying area. The square contains an amphitheater, passive recreation, public art, and other community facilities.

Green Street Type
This local street type offers green infrastructure services from pervious sidewalk paving, curbside bioswales and tree box filters, to system-wide tree lined lawns and medians that can handle five year storm events—the majority of the area's storm events.

2A

Green Streets and Parks: Markham Town Square

Wetland Town Square ❶
Reformat the conventional town square to become both urban park and water treatment facility.

Rain Gardens ❷
Use small bioswales designed to manage stormwater runoff by filtering sediment and pollutants.

Bio-Retention Mat ❸
Incorporate a wetland landscape designed to manage stormwater runoff, mostly through retention.

Green Street ❹
Build streets with low impact development facilities, to treat stormwater runoff, provide shade and habitat, and to purify air.

Evapotranspiring Tree Bosques ❺
Employ groves of deep-rooting trees to uptake large amounts of water for transpiration.

Living Bridge ❻
Use vegetated bridges with phytoremediating and flowering plants, allowing pedestrian access to mounds as well as providing ecosystem services.

Multi-programmatic Mounds (Pumping Water, Recreational, Habitat) ❼
Design vegetated mounds as green spaces for recreational activities while absorbing and transpiring stormwater runoff through tree bosques.

0   60'   120'

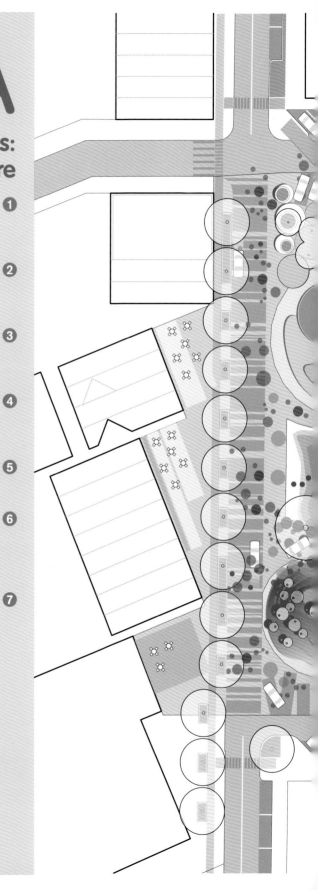

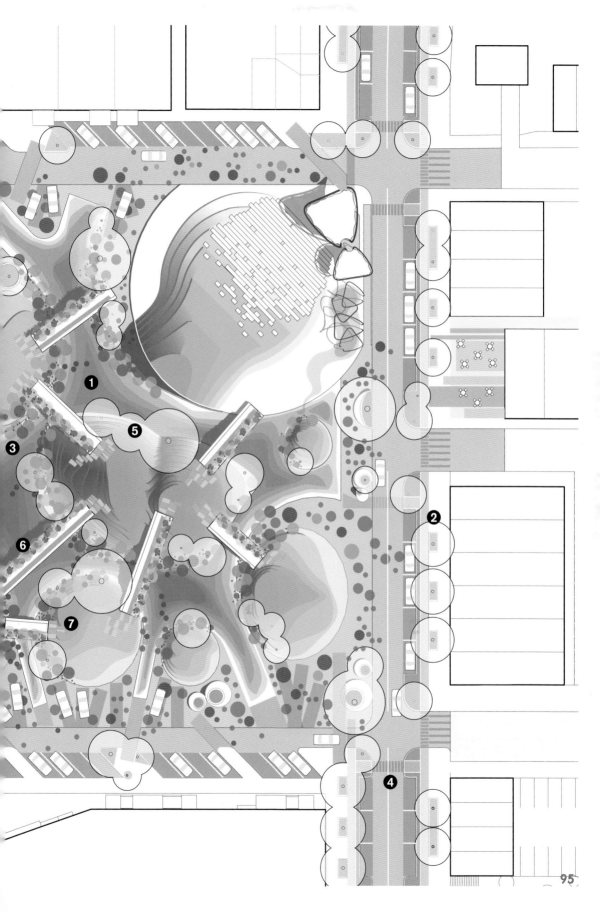

Green Streets and Parks:
Markham Town Square

Underground Filtration Basins are rock-filled trenches with bio-films beneath porous pavement that filter sediment and infiltrate stormwater runoff providing water **regulating services** in streets.

Phreatophytic Bosques

are water-loving, deep-rooted trees (e.g., Cottonwoods, Poplars, Willows, etc.) that provide flow **regulating services** by pumping, storing, and evapotranspiring groundwater where a high water table limits runoff retention. An acre of these trees can pump more than a million gallons of water annually.

Green Streets and Parks:
Markham Town Square

Town Square as a Rain Terrain

Rain terrains are green infrastructure based on holding water versus *riparian corridors* based on drainage. Rain terrains prevent uncontrolled flooding in urbanized areas by managing overflow, and attenuating peak flows to streams that cause downstream flooding after rainfall.

Bio-Retention Mat

holds floodwater during large scale rain events providing a **regulating service** as well as retaining civic functions despite flood events.

Green Streets and Parks: Markham Town Square

Reedy Plant Guilds
tolerate inundation, thrive in hydric soils, and are ideal for erosion and water flow control in providing **regulating services**, while offering **supporting services** through land-water nutrient cycling and refugia provisioning.

Living Bridge
akin to a "living wall," supports a vegetated wire mesh of pollinating plant guilds that offer **supporting services**, and **provisioning services** if edible plant guilds are used.

Green Streets and Parks: Markham Town Square

Infiltration Mounds
filled with moss-lined rock and/or structural soil with high porosity provide **regulating services** through stormwater runoff infiltration, treatment, and storage in a flood-prone area of the city with a high water table.

2B

Green Streets and Parks: Shared Street Type

Rain Gardens ❶
Incorporate small bioswales designed to manage stormwater runoff by filtering sediment and pollutants.

Pervious Paving ❷
Design pavement to allow water infiltration for groundwater recharge.

Evapotranspiring Tree Bosques ❸
Use groves of deep-rooting trees to uptake large amounts of water for transpiration. Trees mitigate heat island effect and lower ambient summer temperatures.

Streets as economic enhancers

Streets as places f

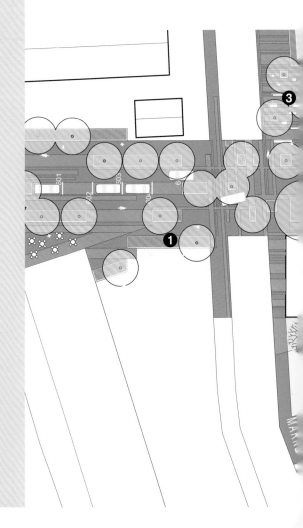

0   60'   120'

1 Fayetteville, AR
2 Paris, France
3 Eugene, OR
4 Eugene, OR
5 Brooklyn, NY

Streets as multi-modal facilities

Streets as ecological assets

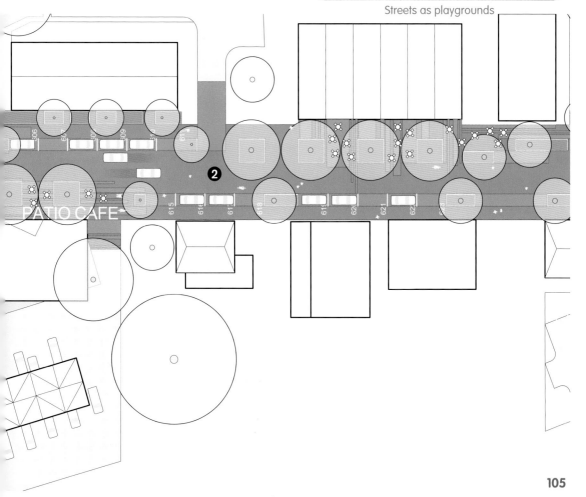

Streets as playgrounds

PATIO CAFE

2C

Green Streets and Parks: Green Alley Type

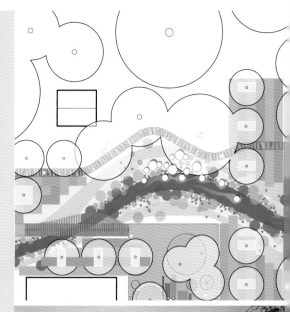

Restore Stream Sinuosity ❶
When feasible, reclaim the stream's riffle-pool-glide natural algorithm.

Daylighting/Deconcretizing Stream ❷
Uncover piped streams and remove conveyance structures to restore natural stream sinuosity and riparian vegetation.

Evapotranspiring Tree Bosques ❸
Use groves of deep-rooting trees to uptake large amounts of water for transpiration and groundwater management.

Sediment Traps ❹
Deploy a system of porous spheres that also support a boardwalk designed to trap sediment.

Filtration Boardwalk ❺
Equip boardwalk with undercarriage filter to trap sediment while serving as a platform for navigating wetland areas.

0   60'   120'

Typical Stream Channel

106

Channel Retrofit Gardens

introduce biologically active zones into urban streams that have undergone hard-engineered drainage solutions. The gardens comprise submergent and emergent plant guilds whose growth is controlled through structural meshes akin *to espaliers*. Cellular meshworks provide flow attenuation and restoration of sinuosity in flow patterns important for water **regulating services.** Plant guilds support microbial communities in root zones for water treatment, and the return of nutrient cycling, refugia, and food provisioning in riparian zones constituting **supporting services** and **provisioning services.** Meshworks are sculpted—and lighted—as signature retrofit installations to provide **cultural services.**

The conventional parking lot is made entirely from impervious surfacing and fails to deliver ecological services. Large lots like this are primary sources of polluted stormwater runoff leading to urban stream syndrome. Since the lot is oversized and fully used only during the holiday shopping season why not also make it a garden?

the Framework Plan's third tool parks the car in its own treatment facility

Students love parking in the garden at UCA. This demonstration parking garden was developed under the sponsorship of Arkansas Natural Resource Commission's Nonpoint Source Pollution Program—the first project under this Framework Plan. Parking stalls are made from pervious paving with gravel basins as sediment filters that slow, soak, and spread water to adjacent vegetated treatment swales. This lot never floods and it is an appealing visual and educational amenity.

University of Central Arkansas Green Parking Lot
UA Community Design Center + Department of Biological and Agricultural Engineering

Parking Garden

Why not park the car in its own treatment facility? Parking lots can be easily designed as productive landscapes to remediate water pollution and manage urban runoff on site.

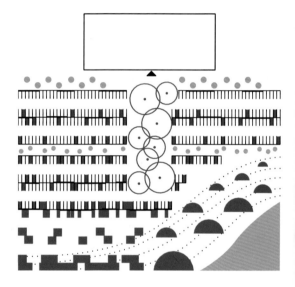

Bioswales

Sediment Trap Basin

Rain Gardens

Promenade Garden

Level Spreaders

Parking Garden

How might the "park" in [park]ing be foregrounded? Consider the Conway Expo Center and Fairgrounds' chip seal and unpaved parking lot, equivalent in area to eight football fields. It is similar in scale to other commercial parking facilities in Conway. Construct lots as gardens using a vocabulary of elements that manage water flows while creating enjoyable places.

Then

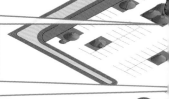

Habitat Mounds and Rain Gardens
Habitat mounds function as flow diverters, attenuating stormwater runoff flows and eventually capturing some runoff for evapotranspiration. Mounds provide wildlife habitat. Rain gardens on the receiving side of the mounds intercept, treat, and infiltrate urban runoff.

Level Spreaders
Tear the asphalt and plant a garden in the seams separating parking rows. Level spreaders slow, spread, and soak by converting concentrated urban runoff from large surface areas into uniform sheet flow while also functioning as sediment filters to trap suspended solids.

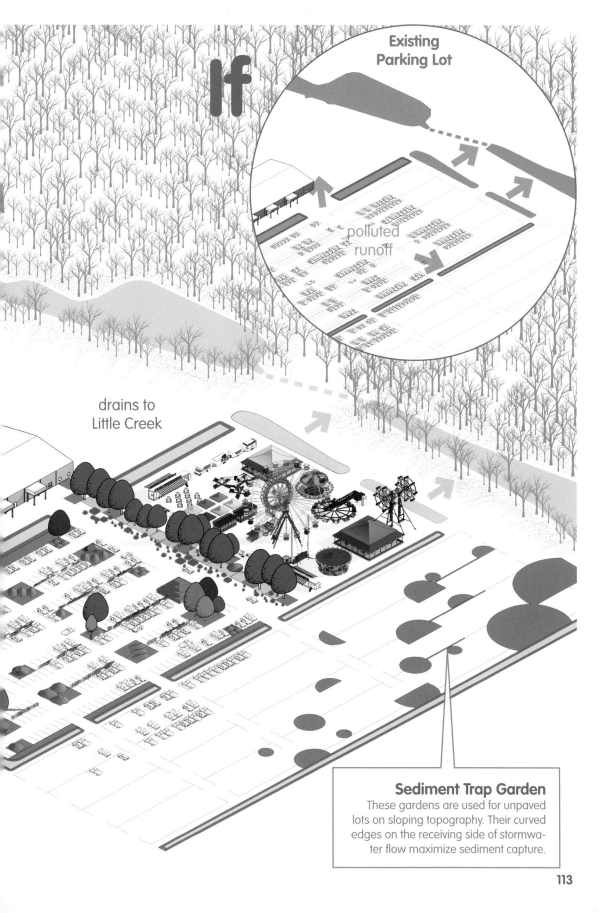

If

Existing Parking Lot

polluted runoff

drains to Little Creek

Sediment Trap Garden
These gardens are used for unpaved lots on sloping topography. Their curved edges on the receiving side of stormwater flow maximize sediment capture.

Parking Garden

Bioswale ❶
Incorporate vegetated channels designed for treatment and conveyance of stormwater runoff.

Sediment Filter ❷
Align edge of bioswales with basins that capture suspended solids in stormwater runoff.

Level Spreaders ❸
Distribute vegetated sediment trenches throughout lot to transform erosive energy of turbulent stormwater runoff into uniform sheet flow.

Habitat Mounds ❹
Distribute vegetative mounds throughout lot to attenuate stormwater runoff through absorption and evapotranspiration while providing wildlife habitat.

Rain Gardens ❺
Encircle habitat mounds with shallow vegetated depressions to treat stormwater runoff.

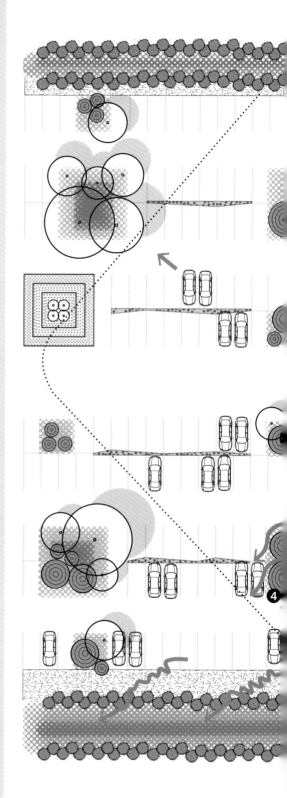

0   55'   110'

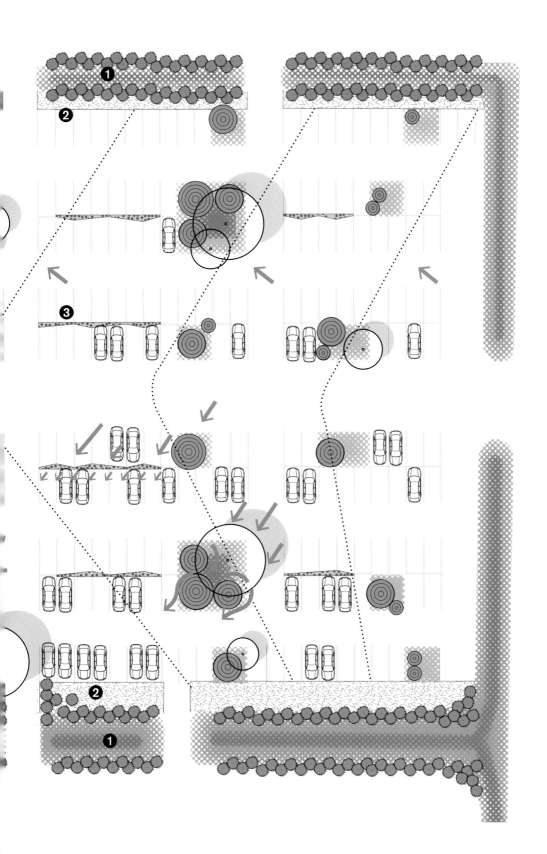

Parking Garden

Bioswales
as flow conveyance structures control erosion, and water volume and quality providing **regulating services,** while offering **supporting services** through nutrient cycling and expanded habitat.

...another rain terrain

Habitat Mounds and Rain Gardens provide water **regulating services** by diverting peak flow energy and treating stormwater runoff in bioswales and infiltration trenches. Mounds provide refugia and pollination **supporting services.**

RITTERS

Parking Garden Tools: Habitat Mounds and Rain Gardens

Ecological-based LID management technologies are designed with permissive tolerances based on in-house road crew construction standards—what we call "Bobcat Artists." Mound sizes are based on dump truck load sizes and shaped with a bulldozer. Gardens are seeded and armored for erosion control per highway landscaping standards …no fuss.

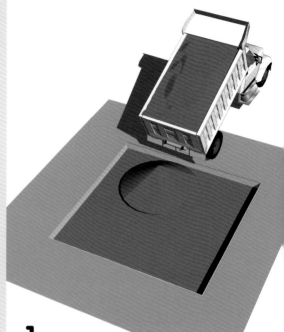

1 fill rain garden area with soil

Be sure to tamp the mounds as you build them to avoid settling later.

Reuse discarded asphalt as a rubble base for mounds.

4 use asphalt rubble and finish with soil

2 grade soil to create slight depression

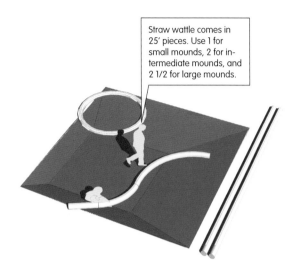

Straw wattle comes in 25' pieces. Use 1 for small mounds, 2 for intermediate mounds, and 2 1/2 for large mounds.

3 construct mound edges with straw wattle

See mound schedule for which direction to shave mound.

5 sculpt mounds (Bobcat Artist Required)

6 hydroseed mounds and plant rain garden

Parking Garden Tools: Habitat Mounds and Rain Gardens

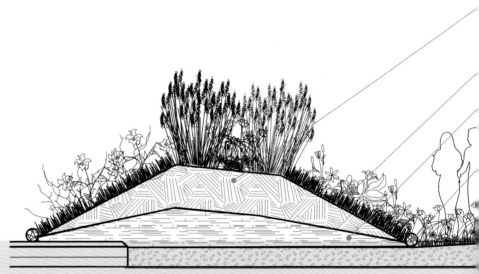

rain garden width 20' x 20' (2 parking bays)
or 40' x 40' (4 parking bays)

topsoil; maintain natural slope (3:1)

plant selections on slope may vary according to north/south orientation

rubble base layer

straw wattle; prevents erosion of mound edge until plants establish

rain garden

Grassed Mound Top

Mound Edge Erosion Control

Rain Garden Plants

Mound Construction

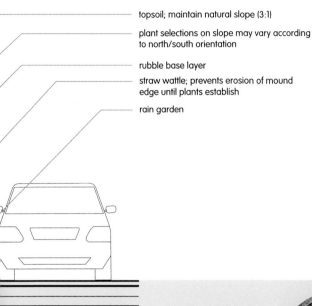

rain garden is a shallow depression used to eat stormwater runoff. A habitat mound at- enuates runoff and evapotranspirates storm- vater while providing wildlife habitat refuge.

Parking Garden Tools: Level Spreaders

These flow diverters and sedimentation trenches mimic the process of cracking in paved surfaces. However, in tearing the asphalt surface to promote plant growth, the soil is tilled to amend compacted substrate for infiltration and planted with reedy plant stock...a miniature garden.

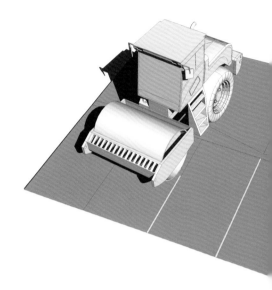

1 measure and paint parking lot

As you till, amend the substrate with topsoil.

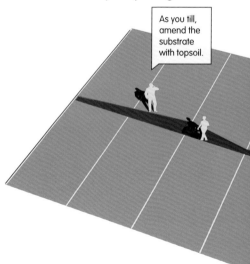

3 till and amend compacted substrate

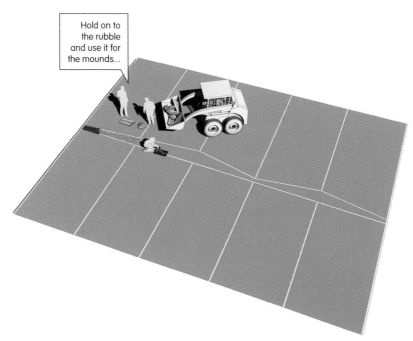

2 saw and remove asphalt

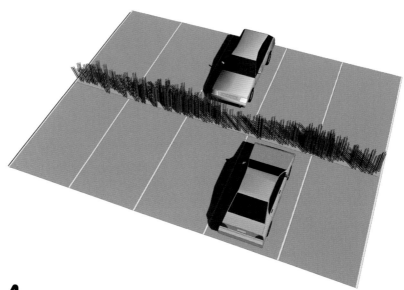

4 plant and fill with aggregate mulch

Parking Garden Tools:
Level Spreaders

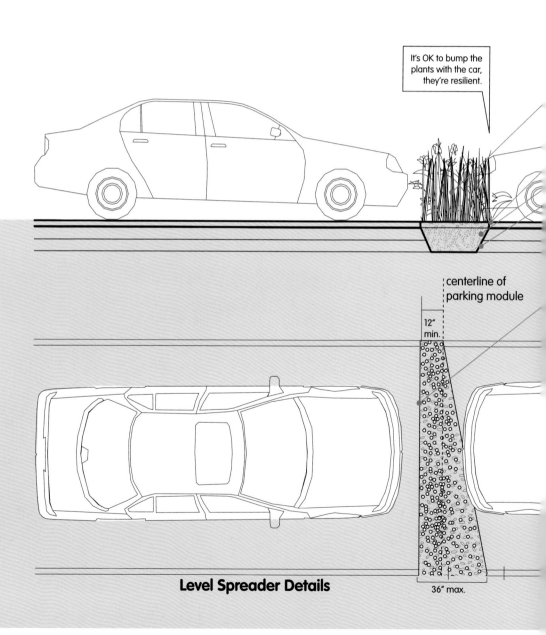

It's OK to bump the plants with the car, they're resilient.

centerline of parking module

12" min.

Level Spreader Details

36" max.

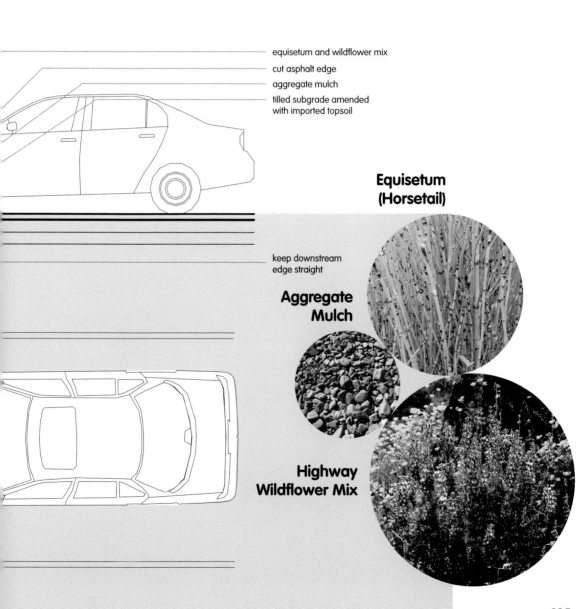

equisetum and wildflower mix
cut asphalt edge
aggregate mulch
tilled subgrade amended
with imported topsoil

**Equisetum
(Horsetail)**

keep downstream
edge straight

**Aggregate
Mulch**

**Highway
Wildflower Mix**

Parking Garden

Living Wall Ziggurat

is a gabion wall that supports a vegetated mesh of pollinating plant guilds that offer **supporting services**, and **provisioning services** if edible plant guilds are used. It is also a wayfinding landmark in a large lot providing **cultural services**.

Expo Promenade

is a tree-lined sediment filter providing water quality and atmospheric **regulating services**, and **supporting services** through porous paving and structural soils that optimize urban tree health. Each tree can intercept and absorb up to 700 gallons of rainfall annually.

Studies have shown a 30-95% reduction in pollutants when agricultural runoff passes through streamside buffers.

the Plan calls for farming while preserving the streamside with a riparian buffer

Conway

Urban Eco-Farm

Farms are essentially energy systems comprised of several growing models between the natural and the industrial. Arrange natural growing systems closest to riparian corridors as buffers to mitigate impacts from industrial outputs (pesticides, herbicides, nutrient concentrations).

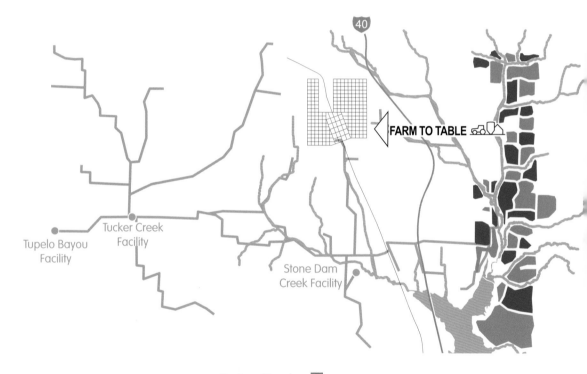

Pasture Mosaic ■

Crop Mosaic ■

City Sewer Trunks indicating area of future growth —

Water Treatment Locations ●

Downtown Conway ▦

Urban Eco-Farm

Imagine a new paradigm for the farm as an urban asset—"farm to table"—providing locally-sourced food and increased economic returns while minimizing production and transportation cost. Such farms are popping up all over American cities and have an astounding rate of financial return.

Then

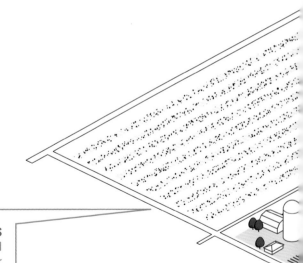

Adopt Eco-Farming Techniques
Restore healthy soil structure through no-till farming, crop and grazing rotation, and cover crop recharge during the off-season. Best barnyard practices include better manure management through practices such as deep litter farming/composting, and manure sharing.

Laminate Farming Operations
Arrange farming operations in response to stream and floodplain proximity: natural farming techniques near the stream; more intensive growing techniques located within the interior.

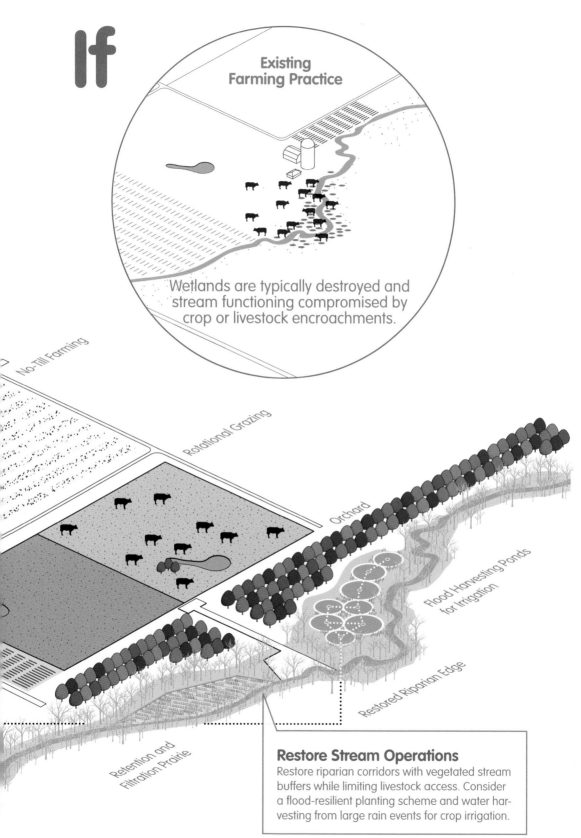

If

Existing Farming Practice

Wetlands are typically destroyed and stream functioning compromised by crop or livestock encroachments.

No-Till Farming

Rotational Grazing

Orchard

Flood Harvesting Ponds for Irrigation

Restored Riparian Edge

Retention and Filtration Prairie

Restore Stream Operations

Restore riparian corridors with vegetated stream buffers while limiting livestock access. Consider a flood-resilient planting scheme and water harvesting from large rain events for crop irrigation.

Urban Eco-Farm

Riparian Buffer ❶
Consider requiring a stream buffer to slow and filter stormwater runoff, and to protect stream integrity.

Wastewater Treatment Wetland ❷
Include a bio-treatment facility for livestock waste including pre-treatment and post-treatment polishing ponds if livestock access streamside.

Rotational Grazing ❸
Adapt seasonal migration of grazing livestock to allow regeneration of pastures.

No-Till Farming ❹
Consider this growing technique that does not disturb soil, increasing water and nutrient retention. It is effective in preventing soil erosion and in building high-quality soil.

Flood Harvesting Ponds ❺
Consider using floodplain wetlands that harvest floodwater for farm irrigation while treating stormwater runoff from agricultural operations.

Livestock Streamside Control ❻
Use paddocks that limit livestock's destruction of streamsides and buffers. Streamside substrates redirect runoff to a wastewater treatment wetland, and facilitate manure up-cycling for compost applications that increase soil health.

Native Mussels ❼
Introduce these endangered nutrient filters into water bodies to reduce harmful bacteria, especially E. coli.

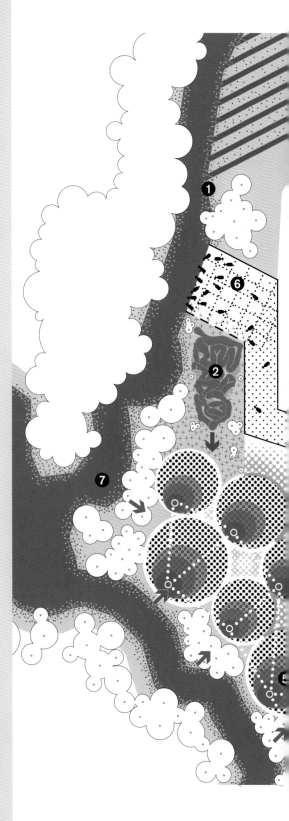

0 250' 500'

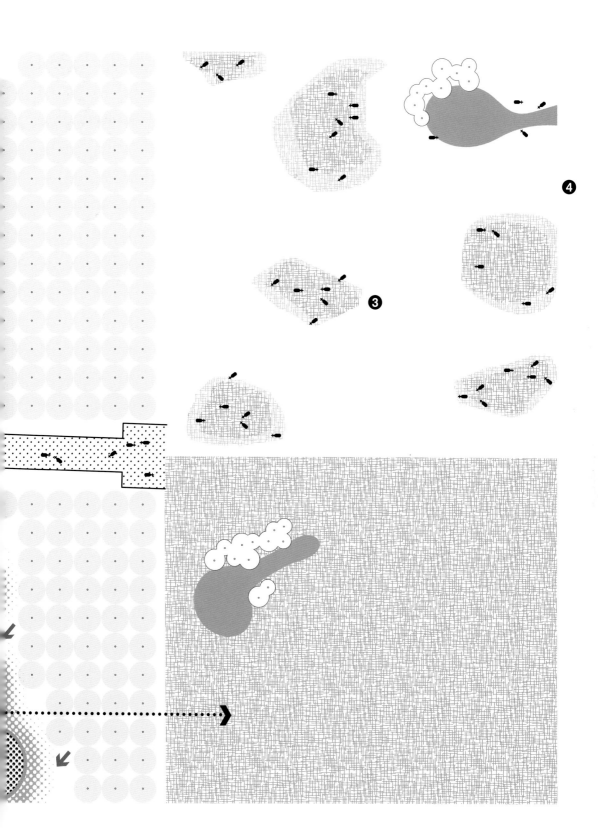

❸

❹

Urban Eco-Farm

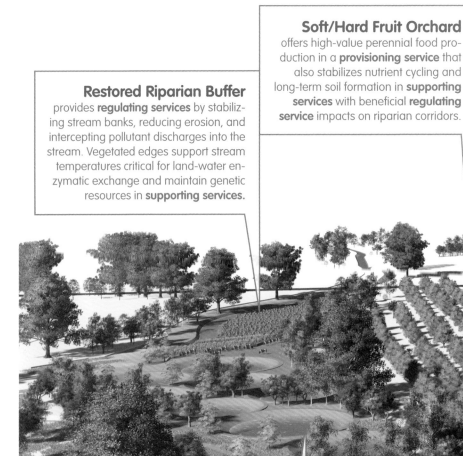

Soft/Hard Fruit Orchard offers high-value perennial food production in a **provisioning service** that also stabilizes nutrient cycling and long-term soil formation in **supporting services** with beneficial **regulating service** impacts on riparian corridors.

Restored Riparian Buffer provides **regulating services** by stabilizing stream banks, reducing erosion, and intercepting pollutant discharges into the stream. Vegetated edges support stream temperatures critical for land-water enzymatic exchange and maintain genetic resources in **supporting services.**

Flood Harvesting Ponds provide disturbance and water **regulating services** through storage and harvest of floodwater during peak rainfall for future irrigation, a water **provisioning service.** Wetland vegetation provides highly productive refugia and soil communities, and is a critical source of genetic material and food foraging in **supporting** and **provisioning services.**

No-Till Farming

provides important **supporting services** by maintaining nutrient-rich biotic communities and moisture in soil structure, while preventing erosion, an important **regulating service,** and optimizing food and fiber production in **provisioning services.**

Rotational Grazing

balances food provisioning for livestock with the landscape's **provisioning service** capacity and ability of pasture soil to metabolize nutrient-rich animal waste toward healthy soil formation, a **supporting service.**

the Plan's fifth tool: riparian corridor as housing frontage since biking is the new golf

Optimal ecosystem functioning entails physical connectivity among landscapes—the very feature cities erase. Where the city and the watershed meet presents the greatest opportunities for hybrid solutions. New types of public spaces should appear.

Conway

Conservation Development

5

Cluster impervious surfaces in residential development (roofs, drives, and streets) to preserve landscape for on-site water management. Such real estate products always enjoy a higher premium than conventional development.

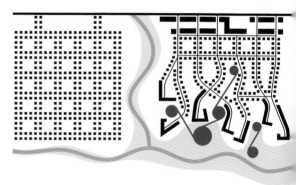

Traditional Subdivision   Alternative Clustering

Single Family House

Town Homes + Mixed Use

Multi-Family Housing

Retention/Remediation Facilities/Soft Infrastructure

Reclaimed Floodplain

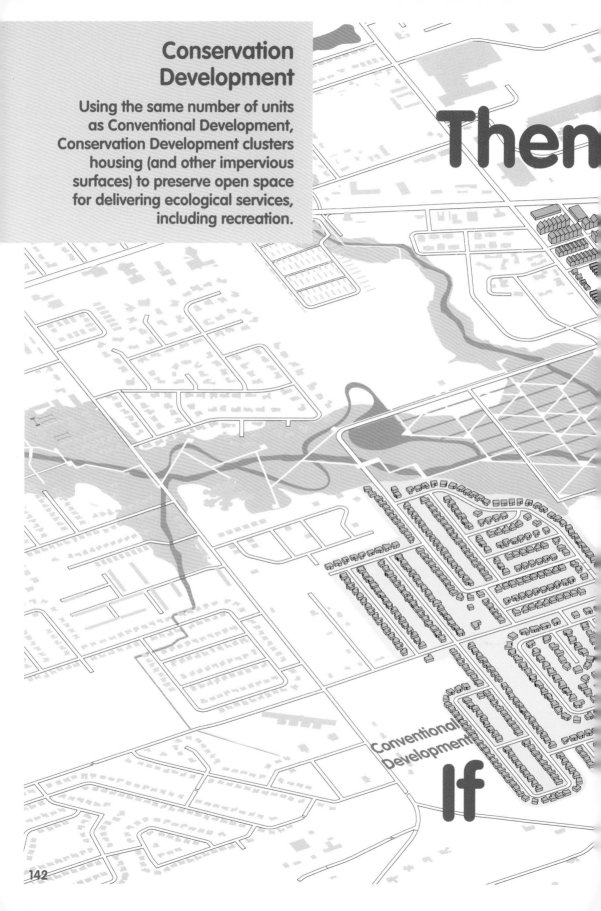

Conservation Development

Using the same number of units as Conventional Development, Conservation Development clusters housing (and other impervious surfaces) to preserve open space for delivering ecological services, including recreation.

Then

If

Conventional Development

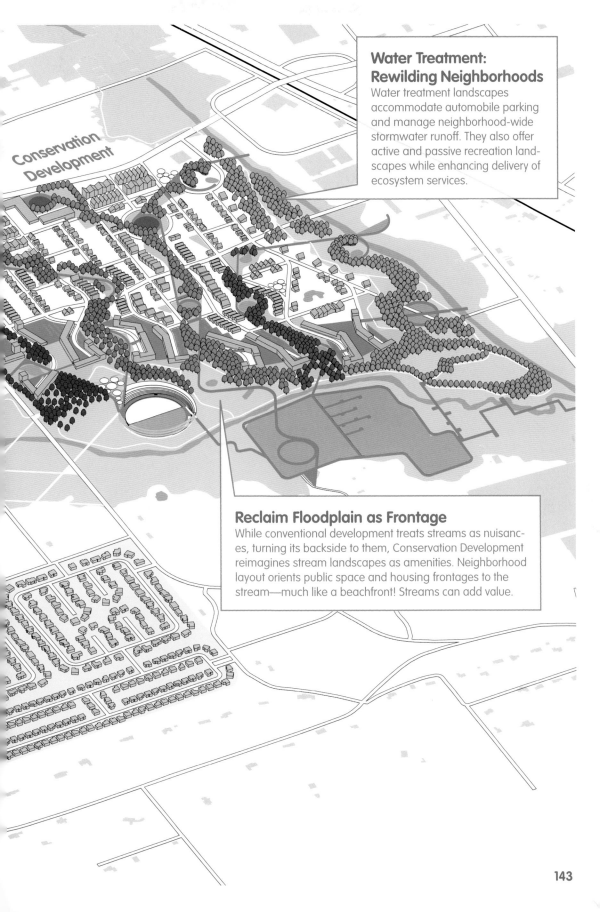

Conservation
Development

Water Treatment: Rewilding Neighborhoods

Water treatment landscapes accommodate automobile parking and manage neighborhood-wide stormwater runoff. They also offer active and passive recreation landscapes while enhancing delivery of ecosystem services.

Reclaim Floodplain as Frontage

While conventional development treats streams as nuisances, turning its backside to them, Conservation Development reimagines stream landscapes as amenities. Neighborhood layout orients public space and housing frontages to the stream—much like a beachfront! Streams can add value.

Conservation Development

Restored Riparian Corridor ①
Improve riparian stream buffer to optimize stream protection and create a neighborhood amenity.

Water Retention Ponds ②
Develop a pond system to capture and treat stormwater runoff.

Filtration Meadow ③
Consider using meadows in disturbance regulation to absorb floodwaters and filter sediment.

Neighborhood Drifts ④
Employ clustered landscapes that combine parking and recreation with stormwater management and wildlife habitat.

Retention Meadow (wet/dry) ⑤
Improve riparian corridor with a wet meadow for stormwater management.

Waterfront Recreational Amenities ⑥
Reclaim the floodplain's intrinsic suitabilities for recreation.

Parking Gardens ⑦
Incorporate parking facilities in neighborhood drifts incorporating low impact development techniques to manage stormwater runoff.

Native Mussels ⑧
Introduce these endangered nutrient filters into water bodies to reduce harmful bacteria, especially E. coli.

0   600'   1200'

Conservation Development

Vegetated Riparian Bank combines **regulating** and **cultural services** by capitalizing on the intrinsic aesthetics of the floodplain as residential frontage, protecting riparian functioning while increasing property values.

Floodplain Terraces reconstruct wetland plant communities at the decommissioned waste water treatment plant providing water and disturbance **regulating services,** while offering **cultural services** through recreational amenities.

City Greenway
protects the riparian landscape as a continuous ecosystem for optimum recreational
and watershed functioning that provide **provisioning** and **cultural services,** including
continuous wildlife corridors and sustained
genetic diversity in **supporting services.**

Neighborhood Drifts
combine linear remediation landscapes for auto parking, providing
water and disturbance **regulating
services,** with wildlife corridors and ex-
tensive habitat as **supporting services.**

Conway has great bones for developing a prized greenway system

For the city to work like a sponge, greenways can readily employ Low Impact Development techniques, riparian corridor improvements, and green infrastructure. These tools slow, soak, and spread urban runoff through landscape systems, given their intrinsic capacity for biologic treatment and metabolization of contaminants...and they can be inspiring cityscapes.

Conway

Exemplar: Davis, CA

City Greenway

Build an alternative pedestrian and bicycle transportation network through green right-of-way improvements to riparian corridors and streets that enhance water management. Create the network from micro-loops for ease of implementation and use.

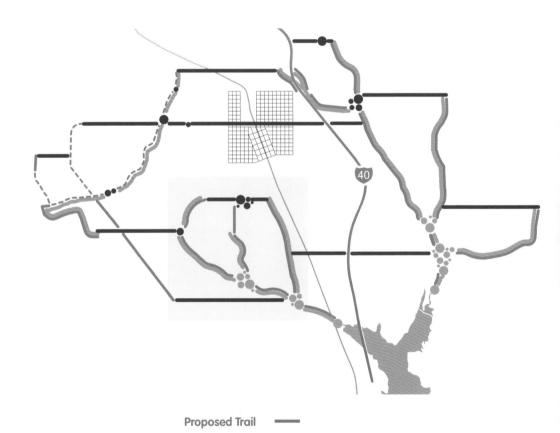

Proposed Trail	——
Existing Trail	- - -
Green Street Connectors	▬▬
City Parks	●●
Wetlands	●●

City Greenway

Streets and streams can be combined into a shared network through a greenway that improves the ecological footprint of both systems. The greenway as a linear park connects existing City parks offering a public sector catalyst for thoughtful development.

UCA Campus
6A

6B
Urban Floodplain Park

Create a Riparian Trail
Use trail facilities, including boardwalks, to restore riparian zones through structures that address bank armoring, filtration, velocity control, and water access. Every investment in a path or structure should enhance water management functions.

Building a Network through Loops
Selectively add green street improvements with bike facilities where possible and complete loops started within riparian corridors. These loops could define neighborhood identity and satisfy open space requirements.

City
Ballpark

Conservation
Development

Treatment
Facility

6C
Wetland
Preserve Park

Connect City Greens/Parks
Riparian environments can be extended into city recreational spaces like ballparks, campuses/schools, wetland parks, and various city greens/parks so that all may deliver water treatment functions.

153

6A

City Greenway: UCA Campus

Restored Riparian Corridor ❶
Employ corridor improvements in tandem with transportation facilities for pedestrians and cyclists.

Living Wall ❷
Retrofit concrete walls on riparian edge with a vertical garden in lieu of removing walls (typical).

Cooling Water Bosques ❸
Locate tree clusters near a water body to regulate stream temperature.

Parking Gardens ❹
Retrofit parking facilities with low impact development technologies to manage stormwater runoff.

Bridges with Flow Control ❺
Equip bridges with functions in their undercarriage to dissipate flow energy during flood events.

Natural Bank Armoring ❻
Remove the concrete edge and restore the stream's natural sinuosity, banks, and vegetation.

Native Mussels ❼
Introduce these endangered nutrient filters into water bodies to reduce harmful bacteria, especially E. coli.

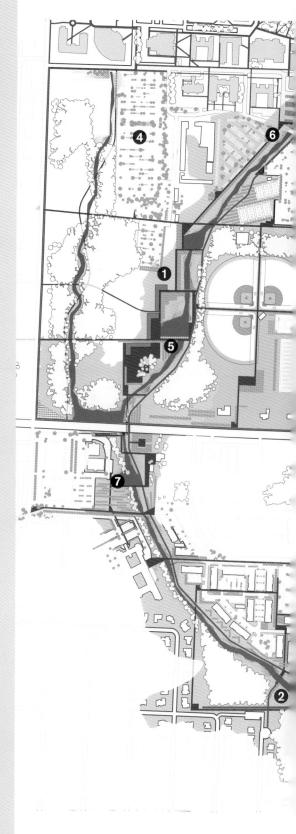

0   600'   1200'

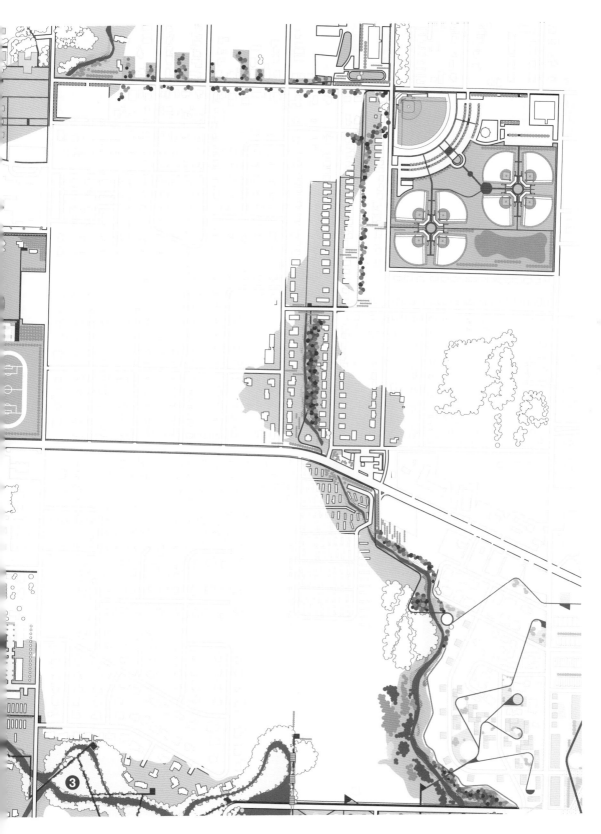

City Greenway:
UCA Campus

Boardwalk Check Dams
provide water flow **regulating services** by slowing, spreading, and storing stormwater runoff in retention ponds where sedimentation and groundwater recharge is facilitated. Boardwalk filters sediment as it flows though structure.

Urban Floodplain Meadow
provides **regulating services** by reducing water velocity and spreading flood waters in a wet meadow while controlling erosion and facilitating sedimentation. The wetland environment delivers a full range of hydrological services amidst recreational amenities as a **cultural service.**

6B

City Greenway: Urban Floodplain Park

Restored Riparian Corridor ❶
Restore thalweg sinuosity, bankfull, vegetated banks, and floodplain for full ecological functioning.

Retention Ponds ❷
Capture and store stormwater runoff in wetland habitat as a trail amenity.

Solar Aeration Aquabot ❸
Deploy aquabots that increase oxygenation in water, enhancing aquatic habitat.

Pollination Grid ❹
Cultivate a wetland meadow to provide food and habitat to attract pollinators back to the city.

Bald Cypress Bosque ❺
Install bald cypress groves in flood-prone areas to provide air and water purification services.

Oxygenating Riffles ❻
Restore streambed sinuosity and texturing to increase oxygenation in water, enhancing aquatic habitat.

Native Mussels ❼
Introduce these endangered nutrient filters into water bodies to reduce harmful bacteria, especially E. coli.

0   600'   1200'

City Greenway: Floodplain Park

Bird Rookery

provides habitat for pollinators and small water-loving birds whose distributed waste also provides nutrient-rich inputs for healthy soil formation, all providing key **supporting services.**

Floodplain Runnels

are narrow channels for small-scale water flow control that maintain distributed supply akin to irrigation in **regulating services** that prevent quick evaporation, while providing niche habitat and nutrient cycling in **supporting services.** They are particularly useful in low-pulse periods of the dry season.

Sediment Trap Boardwalk

provides water **regulating services** by filtering sediment and attached pollutants in this recycling pathway downstream from urban and industrial land uses. Sedimentation is the most prevalent and damaging pollution in North American streams.

Pollinating Plant Guilds

including Milkweed (a host for the Monarch butterfly) encourage revival of pollination in this critical **supporting service** provided by bees, hummingbirds, bats, and other insects such as butterflies. Wild bee populations have declined as much as 96% along with 90% of the Monarch butterfly population. The **provisioning** of many vegetables, nuts, fruits like blueberries, almonds, chocolate, and coffee all depend on pollinators.

Floodplain Park

provides **supporting, regulating,** and **provisioning services** of a wetland through the creation of a rich pollinator habitat, food source, water flow control and disturbance regulation. Muddy areas, dead wood, reeds, and grasses provide essential nesting areas while wildflowers provide a food source.

City Greenway: Reclaimed Water Treatment Plant

Bat Tower

attracts bat colonies important for integrated pest management (each bat can consume 1,000 mosquitoes per evening) while their "droppings" or guano provide a valuable fertilizer for fish, all looped **supporting services**.

Floating Bio-Mats

provide the water quality **regulating services** of a wetland, including treatment, and enhancement of habitat diversity and other **supporting services** in an otherwise homogeneous water environment.

Reclaimed Waste Water Treatment Ponds

provide water quality **regulating services** and **provisioning services** through the cultivation of hydroponic plants. The reclaimed treatment facility could support **cultural services** through a community water park with active and passive recreation.

6C

City Greenway: Wetland Preserve

Wetland Restoration ❶
Restore hydrological functioning and ecological functioning of floodplains.

Bald Cypress Bosque ❷
Install bald cypress groves in flood-prone areas to provide air and water purification services.

Red Twig Dogwood Filtration Marsh ❸
Install this naturalized wetland woody species used to purify water by filtering sediment and nutrients.

Filtration Boardwalk ❹
Equip boardwalks with an undercarriage that filters water and traps sediment while serving as a platform for navigating wetland areas.

Solar Aeration Aquabot ❺
Deploy aquabots that increase oxygenation in water, enhancing aquatic habitat.

Recreational/Educational Facilities ❻
Develop a lake head system of viewing towers, boardwalks, and trails.

Native Mussels ❼
Introduce these endangered nutrient filters into water bodies to reduce harmful bacteria, especially E. coli.

0   600'   1200'

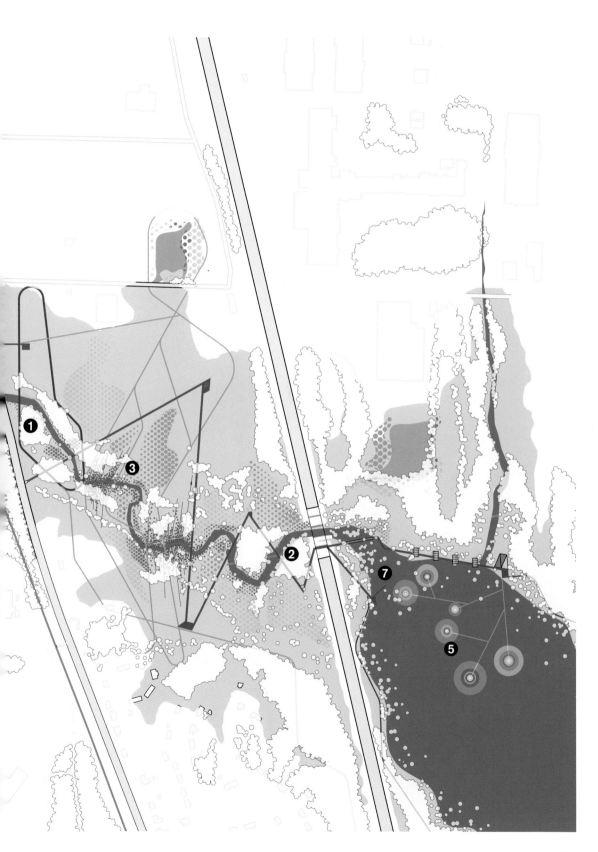

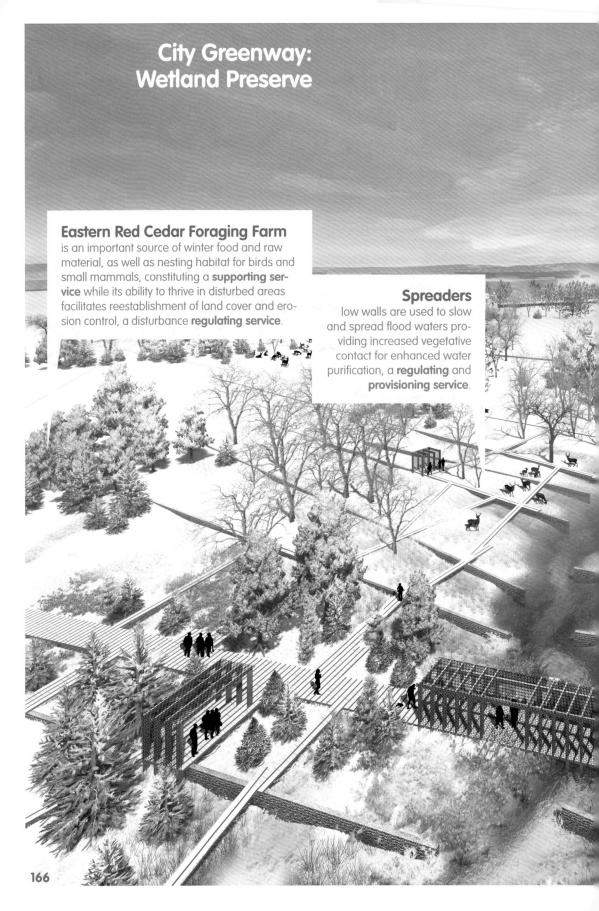

City Greenway: Wetland Preserve

Eastern Red Cedar Foraging Farm is an important source of winter food and raw material, as well as nesting habitat for birds and small mammals, constituting a **supporting service** while its ability to thrive in disturbed areas facilitates reestablishment of land cover and erosion control, a disturbance **regulating service**.

Spreaders low walls are used to slow and spread flood waters providing increased vegetative contact for enhanced water purification, a **regulating** and **provisioning service**.

Stone Dam Creek's Restored Riparian Corridor

provides **supporting services** by functioning as a wildlife movement corridor and habitat for a variety of species including migratory birds and pollinators, all maintaining the genetic diversity that underlies an ecosystem's self-design capacity.

Floodplain

arguably the highest-yield **provisioning** landscape in terms of food, raw material, soil formation, refuge, nutrient cycling, and genetic resources, floodplains also offer excellent absorption and storage in water and disturbance **regulating services**, including waste treatment.

Red Twig Dogwood

a naturalized keystone species in wetland plant guilds particularly useful for water treatment and sediment filtration in **regulating services**, while providing excellent habitat, food source, and pollination in **supporting services**.

Ecological Design Principles

Why not make Conway a national reconciliation landscape between city and water?

1   Ecosystem structure and functions are determined by forcing functions of the system.

2   Energy inputs to the ecosystems and available storage of matter are limited.

3   Ecosystems are open and dissipative systems.

4   Attention to a limited number of factors is most strategic in preventing pollution or restoring ecosystems.

5   Ecosystems have some homeostatic capability that results in smoothing out and depressing the effects of strongly variable inputs.

6   Match recycling pathways to the rates of ecosystems to reduce the effect of pollution.

7   Design for pulsing systems wherever possible.

8   Ecosystems are self-designing systems.

9   Processes of ecosystems have characteristic time and space scales that should be accounted for in environmental management.

10   Biodiversity should be championed to maintain an ecosystem's self-design capacity.

11   Ecotones, or transitions zones, are as important for ecosystems as membranes are for cells.

12   Coupling between ecosystems should be utilized wherever possible.

13   The components of an ecosystem are interconnected, interrelated, and form a network, implying that direct as well as indirect effects of ecosystem development need to be considered.

14   An ecosystem has a history of development.

15   Ecosystems and species are most vulnerable at their geographic edges.

16   Ecosystems are hierarchical systems and are part of a larger landscape.

17   Physical and biological processes are interactive. It is important to understand both physical and biological interactions and to interpret them properly.

18   Ecotechnology requires a holistic approach that integrates all interacting parts and processes as far as possible.

19   Information in ecosystems is stored in structures.

Source: Mitsch and Jorgensen, *Ecological Engineering and Ecosystem Restoration*, 2004

Glossary

303(d) list of impaired water bodies
Under section 303(d) of the Clean Water Act, states, territories and authorized tribes are required to submit lists of impaired waters. These water bodies are too polluted or otherwise degraded to meet designated water quality standards. The law requires that the states establish priority rankings for waters on the lists and develop Total Maximum Daily Loads (TMDL) for managing these waters.

adaptive management
Iterative process of decision making based on learning and interaction with feedback to improve management outcomes of resources.

bankfull
Composite stream channel consisting of the thalweg belt (baseflow) with water at least part of the year, and the full channel just before flooding. Bankfull formation is determined by the interaction among sediment discharge, sediment particle size, stream flow, and stream slope.

benthic
The ecological zone at the bottom of a water body such as a lake or ocean, including the sediment surface layer housing invertebrate communities.

bioremediation
Treatment processes that improve water quality by utilizing phytoremediation or microbial processes that metabolize contaminants in stormwater runoff.

borrow-fill technique
A borrow is an area where soil, gravel, or sand has been dug for use as fill at another location—in this case, lake sediment has been dredged to create islands—an ancient wetland farming technique.

ecosystem services
Resources and processes that are supplied by healthy natural ecosystems and serve all living organisms. The 17 ecological services are: atmosphere regulation, climate regulation, disturbance regulation, water regulation, water supply, erosion control and sediment retention, soil formation, nutrient cycling, waste treatment, pollination, species control, refugia, food production, raw material production, genetic resources, recreation, and cultural enrichment.

ecotone
A transitional zone between two adjacent but different plant communities where a high level of niche biogeochemical changes occur.

emergent plants
Vegetation that is rooted below the mean water level but extends above the water level.

espaliers
The traditional horticulture practice of training plat growth using structural frames, usually to optimize fruit production or to advance a desired ornamental effect.

eutrophication
A natural aging process in lakes characterized by reduced dissolved oxygen levels in water due to concentrations of nutrients that stimulate excessive plant growth such as algae, eventually altering water quality regime and reducing aquatic life.

evapotranspiration
The process by which water is transferred from the Earth to the atmosphere through the combined efforts of transpiration from plants and evaporation from water bodies.

first flush
Initial pulse of stormwater runoff that captures stationary pollutants, resulting in higher levels of concentrated pollution than that which occurs during the rest of the storm event.

filtration
The separation of sediment from stormwater runoff through a porous media such as sand, fibrous root system, or man-made filter.

floodplain
Areas adjacent to a stream or river that experience periodic flooding where floodwaters accumulate and dissipate their energy. The floodplain includes the floodway, which carries significant volumes of flood water, and the flood fringe, the area covered by the flood.

flow attenuation
Dissipation of peak stormwater runoff flows and volume.

green infrastructure
Infrastructure that incorporates soft engineering to deliver ecosystem services such as stormwater management, food production, improved air quality, healthy soils, and atmospheric regulation. Going beyond the simple minimalization of ecological harm, green infrastructure aims to be regenerative providing an ecological framework for enhancing community livability.

greenway
A corridor of public open space used for recreation and pedestrian and bicycle traffic often located along water bodies.

hard engineering
Conventional civil engineering systems reliant on mechanical abiotic structures for infrastructural purposes, like curbs, gutters, culverts, catch basins, and underground pipes.

hydric soil
Relating to soils that are formed under conditions of saturation, flooding, or ponding long enough to develop anaerobic conditions in the subsurface layers.

hydrocarbons
Class of organic chemical compounds that are the principal ingredients of petroleum, lubricants, and natural gas as well as raw materials for the production of plastic, rubber, solvents, and industrial chemicals.

impervious surface
A material unable to transmit fluids through its surface.

infiltration
The vertical movement of stormwater through soil, recharging groundwater stocks.

leaf area index
Characterization of plant canopy density based on one-sided green leaf area per unit ground surface area in broadleaf canopies, and selected needle surface area per unit ground surface area for conifers. LAI impacts stormwater functioning among other plant functions.

Low Impact Development (LID)
LID is an ecologically-based stormwater management approach using landscape architecture to manage rainfall on site through a vegetated treatment network. The goal of LID is to sustain a site's pre-development hydrologic regime by using techniques that infiltrate, filter, store, and evaporate stormwater runoff close to its source.

nonpoint source pollution
Surface level pollutants generated by diffused human activities concentrated and transported by stormwater runoff.

phytoremediation
Mitigation of contaminated soil, water, or air using the microbial processes in plants to contain, degrade, or eliminate pollutants.

rain terrain
In wet areas, landscapes and green infrastructure designed to hold water for disturbance regulation, versus riparian corridors whose properties are based on drainage and channeled flow. Here, rain does not flow, but rather overflows, expressing the complex behavior in spreading and soaking.

riffle-pool-glide
Algorithm of alternating shallow and deep areas in the stream baseflow (thalweg). A function of stream sinuosity and sediment character, riffles are shallow depositories that form between two bends as the thalweg crosses between channel sides. Pools typically form in the thalweg near the outside bank (erosive side) of bends. Pool-to-pool spacing is typically 7-12 times bankfull width.

riparian
Of or relating to the bank of a river or stream.

sedimentation
A mechanical process in which suspended solids settle to the bottom of a water body under the influence of gravity.

shared streets
Multipurpose right-of-ways that create a common space to be shared by vehicles, pedestrians, bicyclists without conventional mode separators like lanes, sidewalks, and curbs.

soft engineering
Civil engineering systems that integrate engineering, ecological water treatment, urban, and landscape design to use biological processes and materials for infrastructural purposes. Elements include bioswales, wetlands, infiltration basins, and rain water gardens.

submergent plants
Vegetation that thrives completely submerged below standing water level.

successional
In both ecology and urbanism, the progressive replacement of one community by another of greater complexity until a climax stage is established.

thalweg
The deepest and lowest channel of a stream marking the natural direction of a watercourse.

urban services
Material benefits that are supplied through urban infrastructure primarily related to housing, commerce, recreation, mobility, public safety, and utilities related to communications, waste, water, and power services.

urban stream syndrome
Unhealthy stream flow regimes marked by chronic flash flooding, altered stream morphologies, elevated nutrient and contaminant levels, excessive sedimentation from eroded stream banks, and loss of species diversity.

watershed
The geographical area drained by a river or stream. In the continental United States there are 2,110 watersheds.

watershed approach
A resource management framework that addresses priority water resource goals, taking into consideration multiple stakeholder interests in groundwater and surface water management.

" But is it really chaos that lies beneath the lines of rivers? Or is it a competing belief, namely that water is everywhere before it is somewhere: it is rain before it is in rivers; it soaks, saturates, evaporates before it flows? If so, then the lines of the rivers are not universal but rather products of a particular literacy though which water is read, written, and drawn on the earth's surface, on paper, and in the imagination. "

Anuradha Mathur and Dilip da Cunha, ***Design in the Terrain of Water***

Image Sources

All images by UACDC unless otherwise listed. Every effort has been made to secure permission from owners for use in this manual. We apologize for any errors or omissions.

Team

University of Arkansas Community Design Center,
an outreach center of the Fay Jones School of Architecture + Design
Stephen Luoni, Director, Steven L. Anderson Chair in Architecture and Urban Studies
Francisco Mejias Villatoro, Ph.D., Project Architect, Clinical Associate Professor in Architecture
Tanzil Shafique, Assoc. AIA
Jessica Hester, AIA, RA, LEED AP, NCARB
Kay Curry, Landscape Architect, ASLA, LEED AP
Jay Williams, Assoc. AIA
Jeffrey Huber, AIA, LEED AP, NCARB
Allison Lee Thurmond Quinlan, AIA, ASLA
Mathew Hoffman, Assoc. AIA
Cory Amos, Assoc. AIA
David Jimenez
Chen Lu
Jonathan Alexander Martinez, Project Designer, Assoc. AIA
Robert Quinten McElvain
Matthew Petty, Research and Development Associate
Linda Komlos, Administrative Analyst

Fay Jones School of Architecture + Design
Peter MacKeith, Dean

University of Arkansas Department of Biological and Agricultural Engineering
and Office for Sustainability
Marty Matlock, Ph.D., P.E., Executive Director, Professor of Biological and Agricultural Engineering
James McCarty, Program Associate

Arkansas Natural Resources Commission
Tony Ramick, Grants Manager, WMD - Nonpoint Source Pollution Management Section
Steve Stake, ANRC Program Coordinator

City of Conway, Arkansas
Scott Grummer, Director of Community Development

Publishers of Architecture, Art, and Design
Gordon Goff: Publisher

www.oroeditions.com
info@oroeditions.com

Published by ORO Editions

Graphic Design: University of Arkansas Community Design Center
Edited by: University of Arkansas Community Design Center
Proofread by: Kirby Anderson
Text: University of Arkansas Community Design Center
Project Coordinator: Jake Anderson

10 9 8 7 6 5 4 3 2 1 First Edition

Library of Congress data available upon request. World Rights:
Available

ISBN: 978-1-939621-81-8

Color Separations and Printing: ORO Group Ltd.
Printed in China.

International Distribution: www.oroeditions.com/distribution

ORO Editions makes a continuous effort to minimize the overall
carbon footprint of its publications. As part of this goal, ORO Editions, in association with Global ReLeaf, arranges to plant trees
to replace those used in the manufacturing of the paper produced
for its books. Global ReLeaf is an international campaign run by
American Forests, one of the world's oldest nonprofit conservation
organizations. Global ReLeaf is American Forests' education and
action program that helps individuals, organizations, agencies, and
corporations improve the local and global environment by planting
and caring for trees.